KATINKA MATSON

THE WORKING ACTOR:

A GUIDE TO THE PROFESSION

PENGUIN BOOKS

Penguin Books Ltd, Harmondsworth,
Middlesex, England
Penguin Books, 625 Madison Avenue,
New York, New York 10022, U.S.A.
Penguin Books Australia Ltd, Ringwood,
Victoria, Australia
Penguin Books Canada Limited, 2801 John Street,
Markham, Ontario, Canada L3R 1B4
Penguin Books (N.Z.) Ltd, 182–190 Wairau Road,
Auckland 10, New Zealand

First published in the United States of America by
The Viking Press 1976
First published in Canada by
The Macmillan Company of Canada Limited 1976
Published in Penguin Books 1978
Reprinted 1980

LIBRARY OF CONGRESS CATALOGING IN PUBLICATION DATA
Matson, Katinka.
The working actor.
1. Acting—Vocational guidance. I. Title.
[PN2055.M28 1978]   792′.028′023   78-3521
ISBN 0 14 046.343 7

Printed in the United States of America by
Offset Paperback Mfrs., Inc., Dallas, Pennsylvania
Set in CRT Baskerville

FOR MY MOTHER AND FATHER.

In Hungary acting is a career for which one fits himself as earnestly and studiously as one studies for a degree in medicine, law, or philosophy. In Hungary acting is a profession. In America it is a decision. A youth "decides" he will go on the stage or appear in pictures. If the public accepts him, the "decision" automatically becomes final.

—BELA LUGOSI, 1934

ACKNOWLEDGMENTS

I would like to thank the following people whose time, energy, and concern have helped make this book possible: Paul Benedict, Jim Boerlin, Judith Carroll, Harry Cohn, Ron Colby, Josie Dean, Bruce Dern, Don Devlin, Arthur Dubow, Shelley Duvall, Andrea Eastman, the late Warren Finnerty, Leo Garen, Harry Gittes, Mari Gorman, John Hancock, Kitty Hawkes, Buck Henry, Bill Hunt, Jacquelyn Hyde, June Jerome, Steve Kaplan, Joanna Leister, Heather MacRae, Jerome Martin, Michael Medavoy, William S. Miles, Tom Millott, Mary Milne, Alan Montaine, Warren Oates, John Prizer, Bob Rafelson, Leslie Raneo, Pat Russell, Alan Shane, Dick Shoberg, Hedy Sontag, Ray Stricklyn, Bill Tatum, Michael Thomas, Steven Tisch, Claudia Walden, Cindy Williams, Paul Williams.

CONTENTS

4
TRYING OUT
97

5
UNION MEMBERSHIP
117

6
AGENTS AND MANAGERS
127

7
MAKING A LIVING
149

INTRODUCTION

The most shopworn piece of advice given to young actors and actresses who are thinking about pursuing an acting career on a professional level is DON'T DO IT! If there is anything *else* in your life that you might want to do, do it. All the facts support this admonition. The following information was published in 1975 by the Screen Actors Guild about the economic plight of their 29,000 members:

1. More than 85 per cent of the members of the Screen Actors Guild (SAG) are unemployed.

2. Over half (51.2 per cent) of SAG members earn less than $1000 annually.

3. More than 75 per cent of SAG members earn less than $3000 a year.

4. Only 3 per cent of SAG members earn $25,000 a year or more. And the 19,000 members of Actors Equity Association are in a similar leaky boat.

Despite these dismal statistics, there are more drama students in American colleges and graduate schools than ever before, theatre departments are being enlarged and improved, and every year thousands of well-trained and talented actors and actresses leave the sheltered walls and luxuries of campus life to flood a market that can only afford to support a small percentage of them.

Being a professional actor is not like being a lawyer or a doctor or an accountant or a nurse. You can prepare yourself for any of these other professions, and if you attain a certain degree of competence or excellence, you have a good chance of being successful—or at least making a living from it. But in the acting business, an actor or actress does not necessarily get a job because he or she is qualified as an actor. Very often an actor's training has little to do with his being hired or not—and more to do with the fact that he or she is the right "type."

In *A Star Is Born*, James Mason says to Judy Garland, "A career is a curious thing. Talent isn't always enough. You sometimes need a little timing." An investigation of these clichés—*timing, luck,* or *being in the right place at the right time,* all the so-called haphazard miracles of overnight-success stories—usually leads to the discovery that most actors and actresses who have "made it" have been around for years, working whenever and wherever they could, working hard, and starving with the rest of the 85 per cent. This is called "paying your dues."

Many young actors have an idea that becoming or being an actor is something that happens *to* you, and that if you are "around," someone will eventually pluck you up and out of your obscurity and say, "You're It!" These people don't take their profession seriously—the hard work, the self-appointed work, that it requires—but prefer to think ahead in time to million-dollar contracts, limousines, and love! This fantasy land is fed to us by the media, and the glamour and power are overwhelming. The myth of Stardom is one of the last vestiges of the American Dream, like winning the lottery.

But put your dreams aside. Being an actor is work, real work. It is a profession like any other and it's a business.

That is where *The Working Actor* comes in. This book is about the *business* of being an actor. In it are gathered two kinds of information:

1. Practical information and cold facts about the business, the things you should know that will save you some time, help you to avoid making common mistakes, and facilitate your approach to your career.

2. Interspersed throughout the text are the "voices" of a wide range of people who are in the business, on both sides of the desk—actors, agents, casting agents, directors, managers, producers—talking about the business from their own perspectives, sharing their perceptions and experiences.

This book cannot tell you how to be lucky or how to be in the right place at the right time, nor can it give you talent. There is a wealth of books about acting, and most of them are useless in practical matters. This book is designed to be used as a reference book and as a source of information. It answers questions and discusses practical problems that most every young actor will face at one point or another along the way.

The unknown factor that makes one actor succeed and another equally talented actor fail will always be a mystery, a function of that whole realm of chance, unpredictable and arbitrary. I believe that talent will out if you are stubborn, if you persevere, and if you have an overweening sense of your own worth. But you will have to be willing to sacrifice many pleasures for it. You cannot be vague or sloppy about yourself or your approach to the business you have chosen to be in. Nor can you think that your life is in anyone's hands but your own.

PREPARING YOURSELF

1

Shelley Duvall was at a college in Texas, taking all the science courses she could because she wanted to go into food research, and then one day a movie director discovered her at a party. "I hadn't had acting lessons in my life, so I guess it was pretty strange. I just wasn't afraid of it." Since then she has been in four of Robert Altman's films, has moved to Los Angeles, and is doing what few young actors manage to do: making a living as an actor. And she still hasn't had a single acting lesson, nor does she feel she needs one. Shelley's story is one of those that helps perpetuate the myth of being discovered through the lucky break by being in the right place at the right time, like that of the young man who got a lead part in a movie on his way to apply for a job in the mailroom.

This is one of the idiosyncrasies of the acting business, one of the funny things about it: you *can* become an actor overnight. It is like waking up in the morning with a cold; you didn't plan on it or expect it to be there. You just woke up and there it was. And maybe the only prerequisite to such an event is that acting is something that has never entered your head. You have never entertained for two minutes the idea that you might want to be an actor. Perhaps that could be the first method of preparing:

program your head with another set of ambitions and forget acting! It has worked for some people. One actress told me:

I had always thought of myself as a painter, until someone heard me sing and asked me if I wanted to be a singer. I went to a recording studio and met a record producer who said to me, "You're a star! You should be a star! You're a real actress!" and I said, "Why not?" He said, "Come with me to a party. Everybody is going to be there." And when we got to the party, he told me to be nice to the people. So I was. I talked to one woman for an hour and then I found out she wasn't the person I was supposed to be nice to, so I fell asleep on the couch. That surprised everyone. The next day I had an agent, a manager, and a publicity director. I was tested for the role of Gidget at Columbia Pictures, and they hired an acting coach for me. They decided that I was too much like Tuesday Weld and not enough like Sandra Dee, but they wanted to sign me up for four years anyway. But I weaseled my way out of that, and really got into acting. I got turned on to it as an art form and started studying seriously.

More traditionally, actors begin their preparations at an early age, just as Cindy Williams did:

When I was a little girl I used to dress my sister up and sing songs and put on shows in the back yard. And we did sketches in church that were hysterical. I wrote them and got all the people together and got the music behind them, and they were sensational. I was producer-director-writer-actress. We really packed the house. And I had fantasies. I dreamed that I would be discovered by

Debbie Reynolds. She was my idol. And I watched the Academy Awards every year with my folks. I remember Shirley Jones saying that she had been memorizing her speech since she was eleven years old. I was eleven at the time and I thought to myself, Well, I better get mine written."

The problem is that there is no set formula for preparing for a professional acting career. In the good old days, if you wanted to go into the theatre, you started knocking at the back door and learned as you worked. Today the back doors are locked, and there is enough red tape involved in opening those doors to discourage all but the most persistent. The business has changed catastrophically as the statistics of employment (or unemployment) show: not long ago four hundred actors applied for two chorus roles in a dinner theatre in Virginia.

Nevertheless, it is logical to approach your acting career in as calculated and scientific a fashion as possible: for, as in other highly competitive professions, it is generally understood that the applicant with the best qualifications will win out over those who are less well qualified. Similarly, it should be to your advantage to have a solid background in theatre before you enter the open market and throw yourself at the mercy of the wolves. If you are going into battle, arm yourself with the best weapons you have and learn to use them.

COLLEGES AND GRADUATE SCHOOLS

So what to do after you have danced and sung your heart out in the back yard and pursued your dreams through high-school productions? Learn to swim before someone throws you in the water. The idea that actors are a stupid breed of people is not, even in this age of raised consciousness, an uncommon attitude among the people who employ or work with them. One gentleman, actor and screenwriter both, had a telling comment about actors he has seen when he has been involved with casting: "I don't understand the limited ambition of actors, that is, an ambition limited only to acting. I think an actor should try to know as much as he can. He should have the curiosity to want to know what directing is about, what producing is about, what writing is about. It is good to have the feeling when you meet actors and actresses that they are literate—at least in the business they are in. Otherwise, to me they are like architects who build only one kind of schoolhouse."

More and more actors knocking on doors today have had some kind of college or university training. (Ironically, it appears that colleges are training more and more actors every year only to let them loose in a job market that cannot possibly support them.) Most of the people who are on the hiring end of the business seem to agree that a college or university education can be helpful to an actor, that it can give him a good background and some real experience.

Many actors I know have been to college, although very often that fact bears no relationship to whether or not they have jobs. The general feeling I get from those who have spent at least two years in a college dramatics program is that the experience was worthwhile. They seem to remember it with a great deal of nostalgia, mostly for the reason of "total involvement," a phrase I hear over and over again. College afforded them the opportunity to become involved in all the different facets of theatre or film-making. In addition to acting, they designed sets, built lights, directed, produced, and sewed costumes.

College offers a special kind of freedom to test yourself, explore, and learn—a freedom that will be hard to find later in the outside world with any amount of security. College can feed and direct your ambition, as it did in the case of a New York actor who had his first taste of experimental theatre at Baylor and has been pursuing it ever since. And it can help you make up your mind as it did for Heather MacRae, who—whether in spite or because of her involvement in show business at an early age—didn't know if she wanted to pursue an acting career until she got to college and became involved in the theatre program. College can even change your ambition, as it did for Cindy Williams who thought at one point she wanted to be an acting teacher: "I was sitting in class one day and I said to myself, There is no way on the face of God's earth I will ever make a good acting teacher. I'll always be climbing on the stage, pushing my acting students out of the way, saying let me show you how to do it. I think that's when I finally decided I was an actress."

There are some specific advantages to a college or university drama program, even if it may seem to you like escaping to an ivory tower or a nice safe womb for a few years. You will be able to study with good or even excellent teachers. You will probably have at your disposal the expensive, elaborate facilities that many colleges have in their theatre and film departments. You will be free to explore the different facets of the medium and to learn skills that will enable you to work *within* your field later, rather than outside it, when you are without an acting job. You will meet people that may later be good connections or loyal friends, perhaps even the core of your own independent acting company. You will be able to get involved with regional theatres and participate in the National Student

Auditions, should you qualify. And, if you are realistic about the real world, you will be able to pick up a couple of skills (typing or whatever) that will keep you fed and clothed when times are tough, which they are almost certain to be.

Don't feel that because you have enrolled in a college program you have to stick it out for four years if you get bored or fidgety, or feel that you have absorbed all you can get. The piece of paper stating that you have completed such and such a program at a certain college and are a Bachelor of Arts or a graduate of someplace is not a prerequisite for an acting job, though it will help: unless you want to teach. As one actor put it, "I left college three credits short of a degree in math, and I said the hell with that. It's time to move on."

If you feel that you are isolated from the center of the kind of work you want to pursue, you may be able to transfer to a school in the Los Angeles or New York area, where you can begin beating down doors, as well as make connections within the school. One actor I spoke with regretted the fact that he had stayed at the University of Michigan for four years, because when he finally got to New York he felt two years behind his contemporaries who had transferred to the city after their sophomore year. "If I could do it again, I would have transferred. As it was, when I got here, I had to catch up."

Choosing a college or a university depends, naturally, on several variables—what colleges will accept you, what college you can afford, scholarship opportunities, and location. There are at least a thousand colleges and universities in the country that offer undergraduate programs in theatre, and a hundred that offer graduate programs.

Good Theatre Departments

Here is a list of some of the institutions most often praised for their good theatre departments:

Baylor University

Boston University

Carnegie Tech

Catholic University

Cornell University

New York University

Northwestern University

Stanford University

University of California at Los Angeles

University of California at Northridge

University of Michigan

University of Minnesota

University of Southern California

Wayne State University

Yale University

There are generally three different degrees offered on the undergraduate level:

1. Bachelor of Arts degree with a major in drama. This is a broad liberal education with concentration in theatre. It is not a professional degree but will give you a good basis for graduate work in theatre, if you want to pursue it on that level, or for further work in a professional school.

2. Bachelor of Science degree in theatre education. This will qualify you to teach acting.

3. Bachelor of Fine Arts degree in theatre. This is a pre-professional degree, after which you are expected to go on to work in a professional theatre.

An excellent reference book to use when you are shopping around for colleges is *The Directory of American College Theatre*, published in regularly updated editions by The American Theatre Association, Inc., and available by mail order (Suite 500, 1317 "F" Street, N.W., Washington, D.C. 20004), as well as in some libraries. This directory lists all the theatre courses and programs given throughout the country on both the undergraduate and graduate levels, and includes information about scholarships and financial-aid programs, of which there are hundreds. Investigate carefully before you decide. Write for as many college and university catalogues as interest you, and when you have narrowed them down, try to visit their campuses. You have a certain degree of power when you are applying and should use it to your advantage. Don't throw darts at a map of the United States: find out what is offered and what you'll get for your time and money. Always keep in mind what it is that you want to come away with. Pick the program that will best suit your needs, the one that will offer you the greatest amount of training and the widest range.

As I hinted before, however, a college education is no guarantee of success or even employment in the acting profession. Many people in the business think that college tends to spoil young actors, blinding them to the realities that await once they leave those hallowed halls. As one actress said to me, "College didn't teach me anything about what to do *after* I graduated. I went in the front door and out the back!" Another actress who graduated from Northwestern came to New York feeling very confident and well prepared to work in the profession. She quit after two years of making rounds and trying to land jobs, sick and tired of being unemployed and constantly broke.

The alternative? Jump right in. One actor recommends, "If you are going into the business, you should start when you are eighteen. I am against anyone who really wants to be a professional actor going to college. It's a sin to say, I know. But I think you should start right away. If you *have* to go to college, go to college. But if anything in your head says, What do I need college for, you don't need it! College actors usually have to spend five years unlearning what they have learned there."

COMMERCIAL ACTING SCHOOLS

"I got a lot of advice when I came to the city, but one thing I didn't get any advice about was studying. When I came here I knew I was *great*. I mean, I had been to college and had played JB in *JB* and Billy Budd in *Billy Budd* and Beckett in *Beckett*. I used to joke about it, saying that I majored in title roles. I knew that I had something to offer. I knew that I would come to the city and get work. So I came here and started looking for work, making the rounds. And I started getting beaten down, losing confidence because I wasn't walking in and getting the parts just like that. The competition was incredible. I couldn't believe it. I really wasn't prepared for what I got. I should have been told that if I was really serious about theatre and about good theatre, I should study."

Not all actors who decide to study their craft are so self-confident. One says, "When I came to New York I bought the trade papers every week and read them for a month and didn't do anything. I was scared. It's a big thing to go in and see people and say, 'I've got talent'—and make them *believe* you when you haven't done anything yet that will impress them. So I finally decided that I should study."

Sooner or later every young actor will face this decision: for virtually every actor has spent time and money in acting school, in classes, or in a workshop. And for the most obvious reason: many actors are out of work much of the time and have a real need for classes of one form or another—simply so that they can work on their craft, even if they have to pay to do it. If you are serious about acting, you owe it to yourself to find a school, workshop, or theatre where you can go and work it out.

"An artist can paint, a pianist can play, a writer can write, and an actor has the glass, the mirror, and can stand in front of it putting different hats on and reciting to himself. It's like a big love affair. It's just not you, the individual. You've got to have the audience, and the feedback." That's how one actress explains it. Acting school is a base. Not home base, but maybe first base. It will be a good point of contact and a place where you will be involved with people who are doing what you are doing, and at all different stages of the process. There are friends to be made and information to be gathered by working alongside the people you will be competing with sooner or later. You are all in the same boat.

Getting into a commercial acting school can be deceptively easy. I have a tendency to throw myself into things as soon as I decide what I want, so I threw myself into the first acting school I ran across. The school made it easy: the only requirement was a brief interview with one of the teachers and making a down payment. I was disappointed with the process because I had expected to be frisked for talent and to be selected as the member of an elite group of people once my hidden gun was discovered. Instead, I was just another tuition fee. Never mind, I thought, I'm in and can begin. But somewhere in the back of my head the whole operation seemed slightly suspect.

This school was *not*, of course, any more suspect than any acting school that accepts students off the street so long as they can pay the price, which is usually fairly high, a way of screening out certain "undesirables." Acting schools have an inherent magnetic attraction for people who are not particularly serious about the profession, and many of the students are only there "to see what it's like," to respond to the built-in appeals of a social life, attention, fun, and therapy. A school that has all this appeal, no entrance requirements, and low fees can be unsatisfying for those who are serious about acting, since the energy and drive is likely to be different when the work isn't crucial. As one actress bluntly put it, "I looked around the school and didn't like the vibes there. It seemed as if a lot of secretaries were playing around with the idea that they were actresses."

I was lucky because after my initial disillusionment—mostly because of my teacher who, I suspected, didn't have his heart in his teaching but was kind and encouraging in an arbitrary way—I transferred to another class within the school and spent a year working with a teacher whom I respected, responded to, and could work with. He expected his students to be disciplined and serious about their work, and this made me work harder. It takes a demon passion and an undistracted love for acting to get you past the periods when you question everything, wondering what the hell you are doing in that classroom with all those crazy people and where it is going to get you. A strong teacher will help a great deal; and it is possible to find such a person even in an acting school that doesn't have a great reputation. If he or she is good for you, that is good enough.

There are several thousand acting schools in New York that offer full-time training programs of very high standards. The Neighborhood Playhouse has a two-year program for high-school graduates, with a stipulation that "students are not permitted to seek or accept engagements to appear in public, either on the amateur or professional stage, during the school year." Admission to the second year is based on approval by the faculty of your first year's work. Graduating students have the opportunity to show their work to an invited audience of directors, producers, agents, and other professional people. I have talked to several agents and casting people who said that they do make a point of attending these demonstrations at the Neighborhood Playhouse and at other New York schools "looking for the young people coming out of those places."

The American Academy of Dramatic Arts in New York offers a smiliar two-year program, the first year devoted to training and the second to the production of plays, which are performed before a professional audience. Again, admission to the second year is based on approval of your first year's work.

The Circle-in-the-Square Theatre School and Workshop has what it calls a Professional Theatre Workshop, "an intensive program of work and study for thirty-four carefully selected young actors." During the first year, students spend twenty hours a week in classes on acting technique, scene study, directing, speech and voice, movement, and improvisation; the second year is devoted to major projects.

The American Musical and Dramatic Academy "for actors who can sing and singers who can act" provides a two-year training program in both the musical and dramatic fields.

All the above schools require an interview and an audition before acceptance, and tuition fees average $1500 a year.

Actors don't study in California the way they do in New York. The acting community in Hollywood is like the city—it is spread out like an oil slick, with a number of different nuclei or small groups who stick together. Although there are quite a few commercial acting schools in the Hollywood area, the most popular are the West Coast branch of the Strasberg Theater Institute and the Actors' Studio. Many actors study with private teachers or simply do their own thing, independently or in a workshop.

If you are interested in studying in a commercial school,* it goes without saying that you should carefully investigate it as to its reputation, staff, and program, avoiding any school that claims to teach you acting in twelve easy lessons. Keep a wary eye out for commercial acting schools that claim they can get you jobs after you have taken one of their courses, especially those that specialize in television acting. If a school makes such a claim, you can be almost certain that something is fishy. Stay away! There are, of course, legitimate, established schools that offer classes in television acting, such as the Weist-Barron School of Television Commercial Acting (308 East 79th Street, New York, N.Y. 10021), which has been in operation since 1959. Many actors will take such a class as part of their own training program, as it is often the only way to get some experience and some knowledge of the technical aspects involved in this medium. Here you can learn something about how you come across on tape, what is required of you, and how you can get comfortable with it before you are faced with a real audition.

ACTING CLASSES AND PRIVATE TEACHERS

A full-time school program is a luxury that many actors can't afford, but part-time study is always available at one

* Several commercial acting schools are listed beginning on page 26.

of the commercial acting schools or with independent teachers. Classes are held in the evening as well as during the day, since most actors will probably find it necessary to work to pay the rent and to pay for the classes. In the case of commercial schools and private teachers, it is of prime importance to shop around and to make careful and intelligent choices.

The Herbert Berghof Studio in New York is highly respected and popular, offering a wide variety of courses and instructors, and the advice that a minimum program include acting, technique, speech, and movement. The year is divided into four terms. The studio points out that its faculty is made up of performing artists who do not depend upon teaching fees for their livelihood, and this enables it to charge reasonable rates. The Stella Adler Theatre Studio offers classes for fall, spring, and summer terms, and the Sonia Moore Studio of the Theatre offers classes for fall and spring. The Lee Strasberg Theatrical Institute operates classes on a continuous basis, with rates that are slightly higher than most. Admittance to most commercial schools is usually based on an interview and a down payment. The average cost usually runs somewhere between $40–60 per month for a class which meets once or twice a week for a total of four hours.

Independent teachers usually require an interview and an audition prior to admittance. A private teacher may run you a bit more money (for instance, Lee Strasberg has a private class which costs $1000 for twelve weeks), but usually the rates average about $50 a month for a weekly class. Warren Robertson, David LeGrant, Michael Shurtleff, George Morrison, Gene Frankel, and Uta Hagen, all teach private classes in the city.

Most schools and independent acting teachers will permit

you to audit their classes and I recommend that you audit as many as you feel is necessary to make your decision. You will be able to watch a class in progress, get a feeling about the teacher and the students, gauge their seriousness and intentions, and talk with them. Ask a lot of questions.

Most of the actors I talked to were adamant about the fact that you can work as much or as little as you want. One actor told me his method: "I always had the theory that if you really wanted to work and you really wanted to do a scene, you just did it. I worked all the time and it was simple. I erased names out of the rehearsal book. I had a scene that I wanted to do, a big problem I was working on, but I had just done a scene and wasn't supposed to do another one for weeks. So I called up the people who were supposed to work that week and told them that the class had been canceled because of bad weather. That's how you get it done."

His approach was pretty unethical and I don't recommend it, but he has a point. It is very easy to let things slide, get lazy, and let everyone else work while you sit back and watch. You can get comfortable in the shelter of a classroom where you are protected and among friends. Beware of professional students and beware of becoming one. Some actors spend years studying and never get out the door to look for work. If you ask them why, they'll probably say, "I'm not ready yet." With that attitude, you'll never be ready. Because I was afraid of becoming that way myself, I lost my patience with classroom actors. I felt that they were wasting my time because they didn't have the same kind of commitment that I had, and I felt that they didn't have the ability to do any good acting. This might sound ruthless, but if you are in a class and paying money, you should be determined to get your money's worth.

As long as you feel you are making progress, learning, and developing, you are doing the right thing—what you *should* be doing. As soon as you feel that you have gone as far as you can go in a certain class or with a certain teacher, then it is time to leave.

WORKSHOPS

An alternative to paying for classes, which actors find themselves unable to do when times are lean, is to form your own independent group or workshop, as this actor has done: "I've cut back on classes, and I'm doing what I think a lot of actors can get into. After a certain amount of training, you just need to keep working at it. I have two workshops that I do with friends. In one group we do singing auditions for each other. We all studied with the same singing teacher, and we work on individual problems. In the other group we have all had college training and we all have to go backward in a sense and 'fix it.' We do scene classes. By now we all know what parts we are right for and so it's a very practical situation which gives us the structure that we need to work."

Many of the Off-Off-Broadway theatres in New York have regular and/or not so regular workshops, which are worth investigating.

NON-ACTING CLASSES

"I always had a nagging question in the back of my head when I was in acting school and it stemmed from the fact that a great deal of the time I found myself sitting in a chair, whether it was because I was watching other students do scenes or I was onstage in my chair doing whatever exercise

I was working on. The question: What will happen when I have to get up and move, walk from point A to point B? I might have my emotions working for me, but will I stumble and fall when I stand up? I am not just a disembodied head." This was spoken by an actor with the chair-acting syndrome, which is not as rare a condition as one might think.

There is a tendency for actors to concentrate on technical exercises and scene study if they are not involved in a full program of training, and they forget about the rest of the body. This neglect is nurtured by preconceived notions and by economic hardships, and it can be self-destructive in the long run. "I never considered myself for musicals. I never wanted anything to do with them. I wanted to be a dynamic dramatic actor. I couldn't picture myself in a chorus line. It was like being an extra. What I didn't realize is that it goes a lot further than that. Had I studied singing and dancing I could have had a really good part in *Hair* in Los Angeles. A lot of important people came to see it. And I could have done *West Side Story* but I couldn't dance. And many stock companies won't accept you unless you can sing. I don't know . . . I guess I blew it. Singing and dancing . . . yeah, man, I highly recommend it."

You might not feel, as this actor did, that your acting career should include having to sing and dance. You might feel that your talent will succeed in other areas, and that it would be a waste to spend time and money in a dance class or a singing class. This attitude can be shortsighted and limiting. It is important to train your "instrument" in these areas because it will help your acting in the long run, and it will also qualify you to try out for a wider range of parts.

Most commercial acting schools offer dance and body movement classes, which are usually less expensive than the acting classes. Outside the schools, however, most cities offer classes in yoga, Tai Chi dance, and just plain exercise, and these classes can be very cheap and very good. Once you have learned the basics you will be able to continue on your own, at home, for free.

Similarly, classes in voice and singing for the actor are offered in most schools, and many independent singing coaches advertise in the trade papers. Private instruction will be more expensive, and it is sensible to ask around and get recommendations from your acting teacher or a fellow student before making a commitment.

In all your preparation and training, you are ultimately responsible for yourself. No one else can *make* you do anything, no matter how inspiring he might be. And if you are serious and ambitious and realistic about your profession, you will want to be ready for anything when you are called on the carpet to perform. The more skills you have, the better off you will be. You want to be *seen*, and often the only way you'll get seen will be to do something you never pictured yourself doing so that one of those arbitrary people who might be telling your fortune will spot you and get interested. You have to put yourself out there, and the best way to get out there is to be ready to do anything at any time. Remember that you are your own product, advertising agency, and salesman, and that no one but yourself can attract the attention of your audience and keep it fascinated.

A List of Commercial Acting Schools

There are hundreds of acting schools in cities throughout the country. For the purposes of this book, the following list concentrates on the better-known, established commercial acting schools in California, Illinois, and New York:

California

The Actors and Directors Lab
254 South Robertson Boulevard
Beverly Hills, Calif. 90211
Artistic Director: Jack Garfein
213-652-6483 (or 642-8149)

Actors Workshop
522 North La Brea Avenue
Los Angeles, Calif. 90036
Executive Director: Estelle Harman
213-931-8137

Artists Repertory Theatre
142 Taylor Street
San Francisco, Calif. 94102
415-771-6462

Charles Conrad
3305 Cahuenga Boulevard West
Los Angeles, Calif. 90028
213-851-4559

Falcon Studios
University of Theatrical Arts
5526 Hollywood Boulevard
Hollywood, Calif. 90028
Administrator: Ralph B. Faulkner
213-462-9356

Film Actors Workshop
Burbank Studios
4000 Warner Boulevard
Burbank, Calif. 91505
Director: Anthony Barr
213-843-6000

Film Industry Workshop, Inc.
4063 North Radford Avenue
Studio City, Calif. 91604
Directors: Tony Miller and Patricia George
213-769-4146

Inner City Institute for the Performing and Visual Arts
1308 S. New Hampshire Avenue
Los Angeles, Calif. 90006
213-387-1161

Ned Manderino Workshop
8267 West Norton
Los Angeles, Calif. 90046
213-656-1443

Laurence Merrick Theatre
Academy of Dramatic Arts
870 North Vine Street
Hollywood, Calif. 90038
Administrator: Laurence Merrick
213-462-8444

Performing Arts Workshop
340 Presidio Avenue
San Francisco, Calif. 94115
Director: Gloria Unti
415-931-9228

Lee Strasberg Theatrical Institute
6757 Hollywood Boulevard
Hollywood, Calif. 90028
213-461-4333

Theatre of Arts
4128 Wilshire Boulevard
Los Angeles, Calif. 90010
213-380-0511

Illinois

The Goodman Theatre and School of Drama
200 South Columbus Drive
Chicago, Ill. 60603
312-236-7080

New York City

Stella Adler Theatre Studio
130 West 56th Street
New York, N.Y. 10019
212-246-1195

American Academy of Dramatic Arts
120 Madison Avenue
New York, N.Y. 10016
212-686-9244

The American Mime Theatre
192 Third Avenue
New York, N.Y. 10003
Director: Paul J. Curtis
212-777-1710

American Musical and Dramatic Academy
2109 Broadway
New York, N.Y. 10023
Director: David Martin
212-787-5300

Herbert Berghof Studio
120 Bank Street
New York, N.Y. 10014
Director: Muriel H. Burns
212-675-2370

Circle-in-the-Square Theatre School
1633 Broadway
New York, N.Y. 10019
212-581-3270

Drama Tree, Inc.
182 Fifth Avenue
New York, N.Y. 10010
Artistic Director: Anthony Mannino
212-255-6353

Dramatic Workshop
333 Avenue of the Americas
New York, N.Y. 10014
212-243-9225

The Juilliard School
Lincoln Center Plaza
New York, N.Y. 10023
212-799-5000

Sonia Moore Studio of the Theatre
485 Park Avenue
New York, N.Y. 10022
212-755-5120
Correspondence:
251 West 80th Street
New York, N.Y. 10024

George Morrison Studio
212 West 29th Street
New York, N.Y. 10001
Director: George Morrison
212-594-2614

Neighborhood Playhouse
340 East 54th Street
New York, N.Y. 10022
212-688-3770

New York Academy of Theatrical Arts
134 West 58th Street
New York, N.Y. 10019
Director: Philip Nolan
212-243-8900

Warren Robertson Actors Workshop
1220 Broadway
New York, N.Y. 10001
212-564-1380

Schreiber Studio
120 Riverside Drive
New York, N.Y. 10024
Artistic Director: Terry Schreiber
212-874-7509

Lee Strasberg Theatrical Institute
115 East 15th Street
New York, N.Y. 10003
Artistic Director: Anna Strasberg
212-533-5500

WHERE THE WORK IS

2

THEATRE

BROADWAY, ON, OFF, AND OFF-OFF

If this book were being written fifteen years ago, it would be realistic to put Broadway at the head of the list as a place where actors could look for work and start their careers. Today, however, times have changed. The forces that have diminished Broadway (and even Off-Broadway) and seen the huge proliferation of Off-Off-Broadway, include economics (the staggering costs of Broadway productions and the resultant exorbitant ticket prices), the full emergence of television, and the fact that many Broadway productions are now prepackaged in London, or by companies that come in from out of town. Add to this the fact that there is a definite shift in the show-business world: the highly creative people opt for Off-Off-Broadway, or go to places where movies are being made. This allows an actor such as Jack Nicholson to claim he is one of the first actors to make it in a big way by having started directly in the movie business, with no Broadway training. If Nicholson is one of the first of this generation, there will be many more like him. No longer is it necessary for actors to spend years in theatre productions to get noticed.

This is not, of course, to say that Broadway is dead. It's alive and kicking and it's casting, although the lines will be long and the competition very stiff. An actress recently tried out for a part in a new Broadway play and happened to ask the director how many actors he had seen so far for the play. He told her: 548. The number of parts in the play? Four.

The trouble with Broadway is that producers want hits, not gambles, just like the big-budget movies, and so if you are untried and untested, the competition will be tough and intense.

Read the casting notices in *Back Stage* and *Show Business*, take your place in line, and bring a good book to read while you are waiting.

Off-Broadway is not what it used to be in its heyday, the early 1960s, when it presented a viable alternative to the commercial Broadway theatre, a place for actors, playwrights, and directors to experiment and work. This is largely because of economics. Off-Broadway has gone commercial: its productions are under Equity jurisdiction, which means that every actor has to be paid at least $150 a week on a sliding scale, and a show will cost a minimum of $60,000–70,000 to mount, and so profit is the name of the game. And it seems that when the profit motive takes over, something valuable is lost; the freedom to test and experiment with productions that are not strictly commercial. There are currently only twelve theatres remaining in the League of Off-Broadway Theatres and Producers (the League is responsible for negotiating the Equity contracts with its member producers and theatres), and many of the theatres that were considered Off-Broadway have now been taken over by Off-Off-Broadway companies.

Theatre of all sorts is happening Off-Off-Broadway; some of it excellent and some of it incredibly awful, boring, and amateurish. But this is the place where an actor can get work, experience, and credits, and maybe even an agent. Or a way of life. Many actors are quite happy to make working Off-Off-Broadway their way of life, supporting themselves at odd jobs—waiting on tables, typing, and driving taxis—in order to survive. As one Off-Off-Broadway actress says, "I'm going to write a book; the working title is *Waiting*, and it will trace my career as a waitress from my home town in Pennsylvania up to my present job in New York. When people ask me what I do, I don't say I'm an actress; I say, 'I wait.' That is the most consistent thing in my life, and I enjoy it. It may be the *raison d'être* of my whole life. It may be that this artistic acting thing I do is just my excuse to be a waitress."

Off-Off-Broadway is one of the first places to look for work. Most of its productions are cast through notices in *Back Stage* and *Show Business*, so do not be surprised if you find yourself at a casting call with a lot of other determined actors. The competition is stiff, and many actors are very anxious to get a good Off-Off-Broadway part, a "showcase" to which they can invite agents to come and see them. Of course, you will be working for nothing; but this is where a lot of actors are getting started today.

A good way to keep up on what's happening in this area of the theatre in New York is to read the theatre section of *The Village Voice*. Another source of information is the *Off-Off-Broadway Alliance*, 245 West 52nd Street, New York, N.Y. 10019, which publishes a monthly guide to the performance schedules of most of the Off-Off-Broadway theatres in the city along with their addresses and telephone numbers.

RESIDENT THEATRES

In the early 1950s, practically all professional theatre in this country was dependent upon the commercial theatre of New York, and leaving the Big Apple was the last thing an actor wanted to do. New York was where the action was, and an actor felt compelled to stick around waiting for something to happen to him, the right connection, or the big break.

Today, with the decline of New York as the real center of theatre in the country, and with the development of noncommercial professional theatres throughout the United States, actors are willing and eager to leave the city, to go to Washington, Boston, Dallas, or Minneapolis for the opportunity to work professionally in a resident theatre, and to perform classical plays as well as the works of new playwrights. More and more actors are willing to commit themselves to nine months away from "home," or even a couple of years, to earn a living wage ($150–250 per week) in a city that may not be the most desirable place to live in, but at least gives them the chance to do what the commercial theatre in New York cannot afford to let them do. As Robert Alexander, director of the Living Stage, put it, they can "spend the season living their dreams as artists . . . which means to consistently think, eat, and dream their work."

The catch is, of course, that although it's nice work if you can get it, it isn't easy to get. You will probably be disappointed if you jump on a bus and travel hundreds of miles to some theatre and expect to be auditioned and hired. You might get an audition, but you probably won't get hired. However, one director who has worked in several resident theatres told me that one actor volunteered to work for the theatre for nothing, doing some typing and sweeping and making sure the coffee was hot. He managed to make himself indispensable, so that, after a couple of months, when he said that he couldn't work for free any more, they hired him. Most resident theatres cannot afford to support a large company of actors, and there are obviously a great many more actors applying for jobs than will ever get hired.*

If you are interested in working in a resident theatre, you should know about the Theatre Communications Group (TCG), which was founded in 1961 under a grant from the Ford Foundation. This is an organization which serves the nonprofit professional theatres in the United States (resident theatres, experimental theatres, ethnic theatres, and others), and it does so in a variety of ways. One of their services is to get interested and qualified actors together with the directors of these theatres.

Every year they sponsor National Student Auditions, which are held in Chicago. In order to participate in these auditions, you must be a graduating student of a four-year college or university program, or a graduate of a professional school within the past two years. You must be chosen by the chairman of your theatre department to take part in the preliminary auditions, which are held in January at seventeen different locations throughout the country. A number of these students are then selected "on the basis of inherent talent and demonstrated technique gained through training," to go to Chicago in the spring and audition for directors and producers from resident theatres throughout the country. The lucky ones will be hired, and will get an Equity contract for a season of work in one of these theatres.

* A list of resident theatres begins on page 42.

TCG also has a Casting Information Service in New York which "is designed to assist theatres by locating, recommending and presenting qualified actors for work in companies." They maintain an active file of two thousand actors in their New York pool, adding new actors through general auditions which are held by TCG intermittently throughout the year. Drop your picture and résumé off at the office or mail them in with a letter requesting an audition, but don't expect instant results. Because the TCG offices are generally backlogged from the quantity of material they receive, it might take several months before they call you, but they will call at some point and set up a time for you to come in. The audition itself involves two monologues (one classical and one contemporary) to be presented to one of TCG's casting directors. If you "pass," your picture and résumé will be added to their files and then, when a director requests an actor of your qualifications, TCG may or may not get in touch with you.

I don't have any statistics on how many actors in TCG's New York file have actually been cast in resident theatres, or how many the organization has sent up for a call. One young man in the office told me that the files are not used much, but I do know several actors who are sent up regularly for auditions for parts in resident theatre production. And actress Heather MacRae, after she auditioned for TCG, was sent up for the lead in Center Stage's production of *The Hot L Baltimore*, got it, and later replaced the lead in the Circle Repertory Theatre Company's production of the play in New York.

TCG also performs other kinds of services for actors. In their office is a bulletin board devoted to casting information—who is casting what, where, when, and how. They publish a newsletter every six weeks. It describes theatre activities around the country and their current production schedules, as well as an inexpensive annual theatre directory. These are useful sources of information, enabling you to omit at least one set of middlemen and deal directly with theatres or companies that interest you. Most theatres hold general auditions at least once a year, but nothing should stop you from writing to the director requesting an audition, or from knocking on a few doors for that matter, if you can manage the traveling involved. Many of those doors will probably be locked, but part of being in the right place at the right time is getting to the door, not just sitting at home and waiting for it to open.

Cameo
Paul Benedict—Actor

While I was managing a coffeehouse in Boston I met a guy who wanted to start a theatre. He had a couple of actors and he wanted to direct, so I said use the coffeehouse. And it caught on. The critics loved it. So we stopped the coffeehouse and made it into a theatre. During its second year, he asked me to act, so I started playing small roles. We ran for three years in Boston with great reviews, but we never had any money.

Then David Wheeler came to town and started the Theatre Company of Boston. He went to New York and hired actors who were just starting out and couldn't get work. And I auditioned for him and got hired. The first company was Dustin Hoffman, Robert Duval, Blythe Danner, James Leo Herlihy, Al Pacino, Jon Voight, and myself. We started with nothing. We rented a cheap loft and we bought up old movie-house seats from theatres that were being torn down and we built our own theatre.

I worked with them for six years—doing incredible parts—before I ever went to New York. Since then I've also worked at the Arena Stage, at Trinity Square, and I was at Center Stage in Baltimore last year doing *Uncle Vanya* and *The Hot L Baltimore*. And I want to go back to them.

You see, what I recommend is staying away from New York. Start your own theatre if you can, if you've got the nerve and are crazy enough. Or work in resident theatre. Naturally all resident theatres aren't great theatres, but you'll be working, maybe with three or four bad actors but several really good actors. And you'll be doing Chekhov and Pinter and Beckett and Shakespeare and some of the best new plays. Do one play, do two plays, do small roles, large roles. Test yourself. Find out how good you are. I was very lucky because I kept working in very good plays with very good actors. I wanted to do as much as I could to test myself.

When I finally got to New York I was unknown, but I had a lot of confidence because of the work I had done in Boston. I had an agent who was kind of half representing me, and I called him one day to ask if there was anything happening, and he said I could go downtown and read for a play called *Little Murders* that Alan Arkin was directing. The audition was a cold reading and I was one of the last fifty actors to be seen that day. And Alan hired me. It was my first New York play and it was a big hit. Later I did *The White House Murder Case* and since then I have kept working.

Nonprofit Professional Theatres

The following is a list of some of the nonprofit professional theatres in the United States. Most of them are members of the League of Resident Theatres (LORT) and operate under an Equity contract, with a full season of productions. Many of these theatres use the services of the TCG, which publishes useful information about the theatres currently in operation.

Theatre Communications Group
15 East 41st Street
New York, N.Y. 10017
212-697-5230

PUBLICATIONS:

Theatre Directory:
Addresses and telephone numbers, directors' names, performing seasons and performing days of nonprofit professional theatres in the country. Published annually.

Newsletter:
Monthly summary of theatre activities and performance schedules for theatres in the country.

Theatre Profiles:
An Informational Handbook of Nonprofit Professional Theatres in the United States:—Contains factual, descriptive, and pictorial information on eighty-nine nonprofit professional theatres.

Arizona
Arizona Civic Theatre (LORT)
2719 East Broadway
Tucson, Ariz. 85716
Producing Director: Sandy Rosenthal

California
American Conservatory Theatre (LORT)
450 Geary Street
San Francisco, Calif. 94102
General Director: William Ball.

Company Theatre
1024 South Robertson Boulevard
Los Angeles, Calif. 90035
Executive Director: Peter A. Chernack

Mark Taper Forum (LORT)
Center Theatre Group
135 North Grand Avenue
Los Angeles, Calif. 90012
Artistic Director: Gordon Davidson

Old Globe Theatre (LORT)
P.O. Box 2171
El Prado-Balboa Park
San Diego, Calif. 92112
Producing Director: Craig Noel

South Coast Repertory (LORT)
1827 Newport Boulevard
Costa Mesa, Calif. 92627
Artistic Directors: Martin Benson, David Emmes

Colorado
The Changing Scene
1527-1/2 Champa Street
Denver, Colo. 80202
President: Alfred Brooks

Connecticut
American Shakespeare Theatre (LORT)

1850 Elm Street
Stratford, Conn. 06497
Artistic Director: Michael Kahn

Hartford Stage Company (LORT)
65 Kinsley Street
Hartford, Conn. 06103
Producing Director: Paul Weidner

Long Wharf Theatre (LORT)
222 Sargent Drive
New Haven, Conn. 06511
Artistic Director: Alvin Brown

Eugene O'Neill Memorial Theatre (LORT; summer)
P.O. Box 206
Waterford, Conn. 06835
Artistic Director: Lloyd Richards

Yale Repertory Theatre (LORT)
222 York Street
New Haven, Conn. 06520
Director: Robert Brustein

District of Columbia
Arena Stage (LORT)
6th and M Streets, S.W.
Washington, D.C. 20024
Producing Director: Zelda Fichandler.

Folger Theatre Group
  (AEA—Actors Equity Association)
Folger Shakespeare Library
201 East Capitol Street
Washington, D.C. 20003
Producer: Louis W. Scheeder

Florida
Asolo State Theater (LORT)
P.O. Drawer E
Sarasota, Fla. 33578
Managing Director: Howard J. Millman

Georgia
Alliance Theatre Company (AEA)
1280 Peach Street, N.E.
Atlanta, Ga. 30309
Managing Director: David Bishop

Illinois
Goodman Theatre Company (LORT)
200 South Columbus Drive
Chicago, Ill. 60603
Artistic Director: William Woodman

Indiana
Indiana Repertory Theatre (LORT)
411 East Michigan Street
Indianapolis, Ind. 46204
Artistic Director: Edward Stern

Kentucky
Actors Theatre of Louisville (LORT)
316–320 West Main Street
Louisville, Ky. 40202
Producing Director: John Jory

Maryland
Center Stage (LORT)
11 East North Avenue
Baltimore, Md. 21202
Producing Director: Jacques Cartier

Massachusetts
Stage West (LORT)
1511 Memorial Avenue
West Springfield, Mass. 01089
Artistic Director: John Ulmer

Michigan
Meadow Brook Theatre (LORT)
Oakland University
Rochester, Mich. 48063
Artistic Director: Terence Kilburn

Minnesota
The Tyrone Guthrie Theater (LORT)
725 Vineland Place
Minneapolis, Minn. 55403
Artistic Director: Michael Langham

Missouri
Loretto-Hilton Repertory Theatre (LORT)
130 Edgar Road
St. Louis, Mo. 63119
Managing Director: T. David Frank

Missouri Repertory Theatre (LORT)
University of Missouri at Kansas City
5100 Rockhill Road
Kansas City, Mo. 64110
Director: Patricia McIlrath

New Jersey
McCarter Theatre (LORT)
Box 526
College Road and University Place
Princeton, N.J. 08540
Producing Director: Michael Kahn

New Jersey Shakespeare Festival (LORT; summer)
Drew University
Madison, N.J. 07940
Director: Paul Barry

New York
American Place Theatre
111 West 46th Street
New York, N.Y. 10036
Director: Wynn Handmann

Circle in the Square
1633 Broadway
New York, N.Y. 10019
Artistic Director: Theodore Mann

Circle Repertory Theatre
99 Seventh Avenue South
New York, N.Y. 10014
Artistic Director: Marshall W. Mason

City Center Acting Company (LORT)
130 West 56th Street
New York, N.Y. 10019
Artistic Director: John Houseman

CSC Repertory Theatre
Abbey Theatre
136 East 13th Street
New York, N.Y. 10003
Artistic Director: Christopher Martin

The Cubiculo
414 West 51st Street
New York, N.Y. 10019
Artistic Director: Philip Meister

The Negro Ensemble Company (LORT)
St. Marks Playhouse
133 Second Avenue
New York, N.Y. 10003
Artistic Director: Douglas Turner Ward

New York Shakespeare Festival (LORT)
Public Theatre
425 Lafayette Place
New York, N.Y. 10003
Producer: Joseph Papp

Phoenix Theatre (AEA)
149 West 45th Street
New York, N.Y. 10036
Managing Director: T. Edward Hambleton

Rochester Shakespeare Theatre (LORT)
15 Plymouth Avenue North
Rochester, N.Y. 14614
Artistic Director: Robert E. Bilheimer

The Roundabout Theatre
307 West 26th Street
New York, N.Y. 10001
Artistic Director: Gene Feist

Studio Arena Theatre (AEA)
681 Main Street
Buffalo, N.Y. 14203
Executive Director: Neal Du Brock

Syracuse Stage (LORT)
820 East Genesee Street
Syracuse, N.Y. 13210
Artistic Director: Arthur Storch

Ohio
Cincinnati Playhouse in the Park (LORT)
962 Mt. Adams Circle
Cincinnati, Ohio 45202
Artistic Director: Harold Scott

Cleveland Playhouse (LORT)
2040 East 86th Street
Cleveland, Ohio 44106
Director: Richard Oberlin

Great Lakes Shakespeare Association
    (LORT; summer)
Lakewood Civic Auditorium
Franklin Boulevard and Bunts Road
Lakewood, Ohio 44107
Producer-Director: Lawrence Carra

Rhode Island
Trinity Square Repertory Company (LORT)
201 Washington Street
    Theatre: 7 Bridgham Street
Providence, R.I. 02903
Director: Adrian Hall

Texas
Alley Theatre (LORT)
615 Texas Avenue
Houston, Texas 77002
Producing Director: Nina Vance

Dallas Theater Center
3636 Turtle Creek
Dallas, Texas 75219
Managing Director: Paul Baker

Theatre Three (LORT)
2800 Routh Street
Dallas, Texas 75201
Managing Director: Jack Adler

Virginia
Barter Theatre (LORT)
Main Street
Abingdon, Va. 24210
Producing Director: Rex Partington

Virginia Museum Theatre (LORT)
Boulevard and Grove Avenue
Richmond, Va. 23221
Producing Director: Keith Fowler

Washington
A Contemporary Theatre (AEA)
709 First Avenue West
Seattle, Wash. 98119
Artistic Director: Gregory Falls

Seattle Repertory Theatre (LORT)
Seattle Center
Box B, Queen Anne Station
Seattle, Wash. 98109
Artistic Director: W. Duncan Ross

Wisconsin
Milwaukee Repertory Theater Company (LORT)
929 North Water Street
Milwaukee, Wisc. 53202
Artistic Director: Nagle Jackson

SUMMER STOCK

There are hundreds of summer theatres throughout the country employing thousands of actors each season in a variety of ways—as actors, apprentices, technicians, box-office personnel, publicity personnel, ushers, volunteers—and it is here that many get their first paying professional jobs. Applications usually require a picture and a résumé, several letters of recommendation, and often a vocal audition tape. Auditions are held in the spring at the theatre or in a nearby city, in New York, and through the University Resident Theatre Association, the New England Theatre Conference, and the Southeastern Theatre Conference.

Conditions of employment vary greatly as they depend on the theatre management—whether it is Equity or non-Equity, and in what capacity you are hired. (Equity means that you will get paid a salary according to Equity scale, and non-Equity means that you probably won't get paid, or you will get some sort of stipend to tide you over.) If you are hired as an apprentice, you probably won't get paid, although you might get room and board, and some theatres even require a fee for your apprenticeship. Many summer theatres will offer college credit to paying students.

Whether you are hired as an actor or an apprentice or a paying student, it will be your responsibility to check out the theatre's reputation, the living and working conditions, and to find out exactly what your job requirements will be. And if you do sign on as an apprentice, you should make sure that you will have opportunities to act. All this can be made clear in a written contract or a "letter of intent" which most theatres provide. It would be depressing to spend your summer backstage sweating with props and scenery and never get a chance to perform. This has happened.

An actress told me that she got her first summer-stock job by bluffing her way into a costuming job with another actress. Neither knew the first thing about making costumes, but they got hired and managed to pull it off—the costumes were good and they fit. And she got the chance to play some very good parts. Encouraged by that experience, she returned for a second season, but this time the summer wasn't quite so rewarding. The plays weren't very exciting and the grind was strenuous. No matter how much she wanted to act and to be creative, it seemed that the director had something else in mind. He was, as she put it, "directing traffic." This is a familiar complaint from actors who work in summer stock—that the direction is mechanical, that you can't learn anything about acting because you have no time to develop a character. While you are performing one play at night, you are rehearsing another during the day, and you can pick up bad acting habits, tricks to get the instant results required by the traffic cop.

You can have a bad time or you can have a good time. What you will learn is how to work hard and under pressure, how to work with and get along with other actors, how to feel comfortable onstage with different audiences every night. Consider it a training ground, and take it seriously if you are going to take it at all. If you are intelligent, you should learn instinctively what to put under your belt and what to discard.

Here are some interesting excerpts from letters answering a brief questionnaire I sent out to summer theatres.

We have received approximately 600 résumés and photos for this summer. From this side of the casting desk it is discouraging and heartrending to see so many young, talented, and OLD talented actors with no place to go.

Many young performers are spoiled by the budgets and facilities of our college theatre departments. A summer of poverty with a company like Taconic Project is a good introduction to the real world of theatre.

Summer theatre is hard work and requires practical clothing.

One of the things I look for when people come to my auditions is the manner in which they are dressed, and their general presentation, and their treatment of the accompanist. I am also very critical of résumés, that they are done properly with address as well as phone number and service number and are easy to read.

When applying for a job, girls should not wear pants or long dresses; it is difficult for a director to tell about posture, body structure, legs, etc., which are all very important whether acting or dancing. Experienced professional performers always apply for jobs neatly and cleanly dressed; beginners and those with little experience generally show up in dungarees and unkempt; they may have more talent but their personal appearance often causes their loss of jobs.

We are looking for performers with at least two out of the "big three" talents necessary to the contemporary stage: singing, dancing, and acting. . . . No one should attempt to work professionally in the theatre unless they have at least studied in all three of these areas and can be proficient in at least two. If they find they cannot become proficient in at least two, they should consider the insurance business or politics. There are few enough places in theatre as it is. The untalented and the untrained should be excused.

During spring auditions, the producer attempts to assemble as varied an apprentice class as possible, in terms of their particular talents and physical types. They must all sing and act, and, equally important, have a flair for at least one of the technical areas of the theatre, such as costume construction, carpentry, lighting, or props. Each apprentice spends as much time doing technical work as performing, and some interest and ability in the nonperforming aspects of the production is essential. (To put that more bluntly, we've long ago discovered that if an apprentice hates technical work, he or she won't be happy even if casting brings lead after lead.)

You asked about our view from the other side of the casting desk. In no special order of importance, here are some of our favorite annoyances:

1. "I don't sing. I'm just here to read for you, in case you can use me in the straight plays."

2. "I didn't bring a picture or résumé. I'm having new ones made."

3. "I'm interested in the props jobs. Will I get a chance to act?"

4. "I'm not interested in being an apprentice. I'd only want to be a resident actress." "How old are you, dear?" "Twenty."

5. "I have to have a single room"; or "I have a dog."

6. "I'm only interested in jobbing for Bunny in *Babes in Arms.*"

The above complaints are so universal among theatre managements that you might include them in your "don'ts chapter."

The "Star Package"

According to William S. Miles, the "star package" was born in 1939 when he and Richard Skinner wanted to use Ethel Barrymore in *White Oaks* in their summer theatres:

> He had Mount Kisco and I had Stockbridge. And Ethel Barrymore was in Utica finishing a year's cross-country tour in *White Oaks* with a very good company. We talked to the casting agent in New York and he said, "Why don't you go and ask the Queen if she would be interested?" (She was always referred to as the Queen.) "She won't go and rehearse for either of you. She'll come in with her whole company, and I will get them to agree to come in for summer theatre salaries" (which, God knows, in those days were minute. If you got $125 you were a featured player). So Dick and I drove up to Utica and went backstage after the show. And we sat there and she thought about it and she objected. She had played both our theatres and she didn't like the hotels and didn't like this and that. I don't know what we said that convinced her, but finally she turned to me and said, "I wouldn't have to stay in that dreadful inn, would I?" I said, "No, Miss Barrymore, I know exactly where to put you." And she said she would play for us. Before we got back to New York, she had ten weeks booked up for the whole summer because everyone heard about it. And this is how the package was born, and how we finally played Ethel Barrymore in *White Oaks*.

Today, theatres that book star-case or touring companies for a week's run are on the increase. Money makes the world go round and the box-office sales guaranteed by presenting stars in recent Broadway hits are obviously appealing to the businessmen that package, distribute, and buy these traveling companies.

The summer theatres that present these plays do not hold auditions unless they are packaging a show themselves. If they do, agents are notified, audition notices are posted in the Actors Equity Association (AEA) office (165 West 46th Street, New York, N.Y. 10036), and ads are put in the trade papers. The theatres themselves do employ a certain number of apprentices and backstage employees who often must pay for their own room and board, but there is usually no guarantee of acting jobs for them, although small roles are sometimes available, and an eager apprentice might get a lucky break.

There are two publications that come out in February each year which are devoted to the up-and-coming season of summer stock:

The Summer Theatre Directory, published by The American Theatre Association, 1317 F Street, N.W. Washington, D.C. 20004.

This is a very well-prepared directory of summer theatres. It provides information about application and audition procedures, time and location of auditions, salaried and unsalaried positions available, related conditions of employment, etc., for over three hundred summer theatres. Available by mail only.

Summer Theatres, published by *Show Business*.

This publication is available on newsstands, or from the

Drama Book Shop, Inc. (150 West 52nd Street, New York, N.Y. 10019), or directly from the *Show Business* office (136 West 44th Street, New York, N.Y. 10036).

DINNER THEATRES

I worked for a dinner theatre in Virginia, after reading an ad in the trades and auditioning for it. It was an original play, if you could call it that—a combination of all the Gay Nineties barroom scenes that you could think of. We rehearsed for two weeks and then performed for four. It was really the dregs. It was non-Equity. I got fifty dollars a week plus room and board, and I worked for tips waiting on tables between the acts. So sometimes I made twenty dollars a night doing that. You see, how they set it up, the audience comes in and they eat dinner. Then you have the first act. Then the actors serve drinks during the intermission. Then you have the second act. Then you serve drinks again during a second intermission. And then you have the third act. The intermissions are the big thing, and if it's a two-act play, they will stretch it into a three-act play, so that they can have another intermission. That's how the money is made—on the drinks. I'd say be careful of dinner theatres, especially if they are non-Equity.

Dinner theatres are employing more actors than ever before, and certainly more actors are employed in them than on Broadway. According to a study done by Alan Hewitt for Actors Equity Association on the professional employment of actors in the 1970s, the total number of work weeks for actors in the 1970–71 season in dinner theatres was 10,521. By 1973–74, the total had grown to 28,858, which is almost as great as that for both stock and regional theatres.

There are an estimated two hundred dinner theatres in the United States, about half of which operate under an Equity contract. Casting for productions is done locally, through agents, and in New York through open-call auditions, which are announced in the trade papers and posted on the bulletin board at Actors Equity Association (fourth floor). Take note that you may be asked to sing, dance, pantomime, and read at these dinner-theatre auditions.

Equity dinner theatres pay scale wages that are regulated according to the size of the theatre. A weekly paycheck (the producer is required to pay his actors no later than Sunday of each week) can range from $135 for a part in a "petit" dinner-theatre production, to $202.40 for a part in a "large" dinner-theatre production, or better if you can get it. Big-name stars, for instance, can make up to $4000 a week. Salaries for performers in non-Equity dinner-theatre productions can range from "no standard salary, no room and no board" to "no standard salary but room and one meal a day and use of a car" to "Equity scale salary or better, plus room and board and transportation."

The plays run anywhere from four to twelve weeks, usually with a two-week rehearsal period. And the bill of fare seems to lean toward a lot of Neil Simon comedies, as well as popular musicals such as *Hello Dolly!*, *Gypsy*, *Godspell*, and the ever-popular *Fantasticks*.

There is a chance, if you get cast in a non-Equity dinner-theatre production, that you will be expected or required to wait on table between acts, which seems like a form of slave labor, but this does not happen so frequently as it did in the past. You can always say that you won't wait on tables, and you may get hired anyway. If the play is good, or if the part is good, the concession might be a worthy one to make. The important thing is to work at your profession, and a gig in a dinner-theatre production can be a valuable learning experience.

A list of Equity Dinner Theatres can be obtained at the Equity office, if you are a member, or from the Foundation for Extension and Development of the American Professional Theatre (165 West 46th Street, fourteenth floor, New York, N.Y. 10036).

Where the Dinner Theatres Are
The following is a list of some of the larger dinner theatres currently operating under an Equity contract.

Alabama
Lampliter Dinner Theatre
6000 Monticello Drive
Montgomery, Ala. 36109
Manager: L. K. Mocabee
Correspondence:
Monticello Apartments
Monticello Drive
Montgomery, Ala. 36109

Arizona
Windmill Dinner Theatre
10345 North Scottsdale Road
Scottsdale, Ariz. 85254
Manager: Robert G. Boren

Colorado
Country Dinner Playhouse
6875 South Clinton
Englewood, Colo. 80110
Manager: Sam Newton

Connecticut
Chateau De Ville Dinner Theatre
55 Prospect Hills
East Windsor, Conn. 06088
Manager: Gerald Roberts
Correspondence:
161 Highland Avenue
Needham Heights, Mass. 02194

Coachlight Dinner Theatre
266 Main Street
Warehouse Point, Conn. 06088
Manager: Samuel Belkin

Florida
Alhambra Dinner Theatre
12000 Beach Boulevard
Jacksonville, Fla. 32216
Manager: Ted Johnson

Illinois
Candlelight Dinner Playhouse
5620 South Harlem Avenue
Summit, Ill. 60501
Manager: William Pullinski

Indiana
Beef 'N' Boards of America
9301 West Michigan Road
Indianapolis, Ind. 68334
Manager: J. Scott Talbott, Sr.
Correspondence:
c/o Jim Fargo
P.O. Box 7, Veechdale Road
Simpsonville, Ky. 40067

Kentucky
Beef 'N' Boards Dinner Theatre
Simpsonville, Ky. 40067
Manager: J. Scott Talbott, Sr.
Correspondence:
c/o Jim Fargo
P.O. Box 7, Veechdale Road
Simpsonville, Ky. 40067

Louisiana
Beverly Dinner Playhouse
217 LaBarre Road
New Orleans, La. 70121
Manager: Storer Boone

Maryland
Canterbury Dinner Theatre
1111 Park Avenue
Baltimore, Md. 21201
Manager: Joshua F. Cockey
Correspondence:
c/o Limestone Valley Dinner Theatre
Box 123
Cockeysville, Md.

Massachusetts
Chateau De Ville Dinner Theatre
220 Worcester Road
Framingham, Mass. 01701
Manager: Gerald Roberts
Correspondence:
161 Highland Avenue
Needham Heights, Mass. 02194

Minnesota
Chanhassen Dinner Theatre
Chanhassen, Minn. 55317
Manager: Bob Walin

Friars Minnesota Music Hall Dinner Theatre
742 Fourth Avenue South
Minneapolis, Minn. 55414
Manager: Ray Carlson

Missouri
Plantation Playhouse
Showtime, Inc.
P.O. Box 13531
St. Louis, Mo.
Manager: Michael G. Moss

Nebraska
Westroads Dinner Theatre
46 Townhall Arcade
Westroads Shopping Center
Omaha, Nebr. 68114
Manager: Nathan Block

New York
Vincent Sardi's Dinner Theatre
519 Franklin Avenue
Franklin Square
Long Island, N.Y. 11010
Manager: John Bowab

Ohio
Beef 'N' Boards of America
P.O. Box 224
Harrison, Ohio 45030
Manager: J. Scott Talbott
Correspondence:
c/o Jim Fargo
P.O. Box 7, Veechdale Road
Simpsonville, Ky. 40067

Rhode Island
Chateau De Ville Dinner Theatre
Warwick, R.I. 02888
Manager: Gerald Roberts
Correspondence:
161 Highland Avenue
Needham Heights, Mass. 02194

Texas
Granny's Dinner Playhouse
12205 Coit Road
Dallas, Texas 75230
Manager: Perry Cloud

Windmill Dinner Theatre
390 Town and Country Boulevard
Houston, Texas 77024
Manager: Robert D. Boren

Virginia
Hayloft Dinner Theatre
10501 Balls Ford Road
Manassas, Va. 22110
Manager: Frank Matthews

Washington
Cirque Dinner Theatre
131 Taylor Street
Seattle, Wash. 98109
Manager: Gene Keene

Wisconsin
Centre Stage Dinner Playhouse
624 North Second Street
Milwaukee, Wisc. 53203
Manager: Peter Balistrieri

FILM

MOVIES

The mainstream of film production flows out of Hollywood and that town is the logical place to be if film is the medium you want to work in as an actor. It is true that actors working in New York theatres have been noticed or "discovered" by zealous casting directors, agents, or producers, and have gone on to important careers as film stars; and it is true that there is a web connecting east and west, and that many films are cast on both coasts. But in terms of immediate exposure, making contacts, and your own accessibility to key people (as well as their accessibility to you), Hollywood is where you should be located, at least until you are important enough to be able to keep house on both coasts.

Unfortunately for new talent, there is no provision in the Screen Actors Guild contract, as there is with Equity, making it mandatory for producers to have open calls for union actors when they are casting a film. What does happen when a company is casting a feature film is that the head of the casting department will draw up a list—describing in detail the roles that are being cast—to be sent around to agents. The agents in turn will submit their clients. It is rare that a casting director will see an "unsolicited" actor, one who is not represented by an agent.

Consequently, it is crucial for you, as a newcomer, to put supreme effort into getting agency representation. The way to do this is to work off-Hollywood, in theatre workshops or in a group, or to land a good commercial that will serve as a cameo part for you and can be seen by the casting people who *do* spend time watching television for new faces. As one casting director puts it, "If an actor works and studies and tries to be as excellent as he can, someone is eventually going to notice him, and he might not be aware of it. We are always looking for new faces and fresh talent—that's our business. We are not in business to give our friends roles but to find the best talent we can get, and we are always looking. That the actor is not always aware of this is the gravy." Hanging around Schwab's drugstore is highly unlikely to lead to much, but working as much as you can and getting involved with the acting community (granted, this is not an easy task), and getting yourself "out there" is the way to approach a career in film.

Of course, independent films and low-budget "B" pictures have been places where actors have been able to gain a foothold in the film business. The producers of such films cannot afford to spend a big chunk of their budget on actors who command large salaries, and fortunately they are forced to explore and experiment with new talent. *Mean Streets* and *The Lords of Flatbush* are prime examples of the success a low-budget picture can have and of the impetus it can give to the careers of the actors involved. These films can be cast much more freely and in a sense more thoroughly with the producers and directors looking around for talent in acting schools, workshops, at parties, among their friends, and in the unemployment line. You do not necessarily have to be sitting around in Hollywood for this, because many of these pictures spring out of New York (one of the reasons so few pictures are filmed in New York is that the cost of labor is extremely high). But if you have opted to work in films, why not go to the heart of the industry?

Getting that break, getting that "right part at the right time," and then sustaining a career in films is as mysterious as the indefinable something that makes an actor captivate the public when he or she appears on the screen. Getting trapped in a philosophical waiting room in Tinsel Town is something you should be careful to avoid. As one producer says, "It is still dreamtime out here in Hollywood. It's fantasy land, and dreams of discovery are still a major lure for young actors and actresses. They know that a company will do a film with an actor who hasn't had much experience and that he might make twenty-five thousand dollars. It doesn't happen that often; but if it does and word gets back to Ohio that Jane Doe came out here and is now doing a picture with Columbia, an untried actor will immediately think to himself: Hey, you better jump on a bus and get out there because that's where its happening! But you can get trapped out here. You keep saying, 'Something's going to happen tomorrow. I know it's going to happen tomorrow.' And you have friends in the same situation who aren't working and who are compromising. Pretty soon, one year becomes five, and so on. That's the tragedy of the whole business. Contacts are the whole thing. It is really who you know. The movie business is very tight, very small, and inbred. It's not easy to get a break, and it might take you ten years of hard, unrewarding work before the break comes. That's called paying your dues."

TELEVISION SERIES AND FILMS

Hollywood is really the mecca for television. Other than the soap operas, television commercials, and an occasional television movie produced in New York, the majority of all television is done in Hollywood. Movie studios now control television production companies. The television networks make long-term contracts with movie producers and movie companies for the production of major television movies. Practically all the television series are filmed at the movie studios. The point is that the same agents who package the movie deals, also package the television deals. The names and faces may be different, but the company in control is the same. One interesting thing is that there is real money action for agents in television packaging. A single deal for an agent on behalf of an actor can insure him income for a period of years for a successful series.

As with casting for film, casting for television hinges on having an agent representing you who can get you the meeting with the casting director. Basically it is the same business, with some other considerations that you, as actor, will have to weigh in your mind. Are you willing to do a television series? Are you afraid of being typed? Would you be interested in playing the same character week after week? These are matters of personal (and as always, financial) choice. Some actors prefer to be unemployed rather than "succumb" to television roles. Others have and will continue to make their careers out of the television media. And many actors have gotten their "break" through a part they have landed in a television series, and been able to go on to do other things.

Everyone knows that television programs are rated as to their audience popularity, and that if a show has a low rating it will be forced to go off the air. Actors are also rated in polls which survey a certain number of people in order to determine which performers on television are the most familiar to this random selection of people, and who are the most popular. The result is called TVQ (television quotient) and it seems that network executives rely on this rating system when they are making casting choices. If an actor has a low TVQ, it can mean that he will not be considered for large roles in a television show. One actress, who has made several solid films, and has plenty of television experience, said that she has a very difficult time when her agent sends her up for television work because her TVQ is low.

It is depressing to note that systems like this one are in operation, and can be a determining factor in your employment (or unemployment), but it is a reality, something to be aware of.

The *Ross Reports*, which are published monthly, list New York advertising agencies, their television contacts, and procedures (as well as cautionary "don't" instructions: don't phone, do not come, etc.) which they advise you to follow. They also list independent casting directors, talent agents, and television-commercial producers in New York who do their own casting (most commercials are cast through the advertising agencies), New York soaps, California soaps, and so on. It's a good way of keeping up with what's happening in television. (They are published by Television Index, 150 Fifth Avenue, New York, N.Y. 10011 and are also available at the AFTRA office.)

There is very little opportunity for actors in the area of educational television (WNET-Channel 13 in New York). However, if a station is doing a series which will involve thirteen hour-long episodes, casting is done through agents and through individual submission by actors of their pictures and résumés to the casting director of the series. Taped versions of the regional theatre productions, which are seen on *Theatre in America*, will use the actors who appeared in the regional production in the television show.

SOAP OPERAS

All but two of the soaps *(Days of Our Lives* and *General Hospital)* currently running on television are produced in New York. Casting is done through a casting director at the network or at the advertising agency that handles the show, and these are the people you want to see about getting work on a soap. Most of them have a "don't come or phone" policy for obvious reasons, and the amount of casting they are doing at any time depends largely on the story line; their need for new actors to play new parts, or to replace actors that are leaving the show; and the number of extras they require. Although it cuts some of the red tape to have an agent submit you, and it can help to have a contact, a name, that you can use to get in the door, they are not essential. The straightforward approach can work—a letter submitted with your picture and résumé, asking for an interview at the casting director's convenience. It would also be a good idea to watch the soaps, see what the story line is, and what types of actors are used, in order to gauge your own possibilities of being cast. As with commercials, the blue-eyed blond American-as-apple-pie Wasp does not dominate the small screen the way she once did. There is a wider range of actors employed in soaps these days.

Your appointment with the casting director might be a brief interview, or you might be asked to cold-read a script—which is what happened to one young actor who had no résumé and virtually no experience: "I read for the casting director and she liked what I did. I don't know what I did because I was so nervous. I got a call-back to read for the producer and the executive producer, and then they sent me a script and had me come back again for a prepared audition. There were about twenty other actors called back this time. I auditioned at the ad agency in a conference room with an actor I had never met before. Finally, after a third call-back, I got the part, and was on the soap for ten months."

In talking with actors about working on soaps, I have heard everything: "They are death—the beginning of the end; once you get that security, a regular job, good money, all your dreams fly out the window"; "Soaps are brain-damaging for an actor"; "It's better work than typing in an office—and better money." The most sensible comment I heard was from Tom Millott, a manager: "I think that working on soaps is the greatest training ground we have in the business today, because it's the only place where you can fall flat on your face . . . come back the next day and make it work for you. I think a lot of the young actors who do soaps are not *using* them the way they should. It is not the end of the road if you are young and starting out."

I spent one day watching the taping of a soap' and afterward talked to some of the young actors who had worked in the sequence. Several were doing extra bits and were glad for the work and the day's pay. Two were regulars and had been on the show for several years. Both had arrived at a point where they wanted to move on, to pursue other things: they felt they had learned as much as they could learn and taken as much from the experience as they could. One of them told me, "I think there is a danger in playing a part on a soap for too long—to the point where you have found things that will work for you, certain gim-micks or techniques, and pretty soon it works so well that you lose perspective and think that it will work for everything. It doesn't." I noticed that all the actors were rushing off to classes, workshops, auditions, and play rehearsals.

Soap Operas in New York City

All My Children
ABC-TV
Casting Director: Joan D'Incecco
ABC-TV
101 West 67th Street
New York, N.Y. 10023

Another World
NBC-TV
Casting Director: Dorothy Purser
Young & Rubicam
285 Madison Avenue
New York, N.Y. 10017

As the World Turns
CBS-TV
Casting Director: Joan Uttal
Benton & Bowles
909 Third Avenue
New York, N.Y. 10022

Edge of Night
CBS-TV
Casting Director: Ruth Levine
Benton & Bowles
909 Third Avenue
New York, N.Y. 10022

Guiding Light
CBS-TV
Casting Director: Betty Rea
                    Compton Advertising
                    625 Madison Avenue
                    New York, N.Y. 10022

Love of Life
CBS-TV
Casting Director: Mary Norton
                    CBS-TV
                    524 West 57th Street
                    New York, N.Y. 10019

One Life to Live
ABC-TV
Casting Director: Joan D'Incecco
                    ABC-TV
                    101 West 67th Street
                    New York, N.Y. 10023

Search for Tomorrow
CBS-TV
Casting Director: Robert Nigro
                    CBS-TV
                    530 West 57th Street
                    New York, N.Y. 10019

Somerset
NBC-TV
Casting Director: Dorothy Purser
                    Young & Rubicam
                    285 Madison Avenue
                    New York, N.Y. 10017

The Doctors
NBC-TV
Casting Director: Hugh McPhillips
Channelex, Inc.
1515 Broadway
New York, N.Y. 10036

Soap Operas in Los Angeles

Days of Our Lives
NBC-TV
Casting Director: Renée Valente
Screen Gems
Colgems Square
Burbank, Calif. 91505

General Hospital
ABC-TV
Casting Director: Ross Brown
7319 Beverly Boulevard
Los Angeles, Calif. 90036

COMMERCIALS

SCENE: A long, carpeted hallway in a building which houses one of New York's largest advertising agencies. At the far end of the hallway are six straightbacked chairs, lined up against the wall. A married couple occupy two of the chairs. They are both actors. They share the same mouth spray, and keep their pictures in a joint portfolio. They are waiting to see a casting director, with whom they have managed to get an appointment, either through submitting pictures and résumés or by making a telephone call that has reached the right person, or by having an agent, or through some other connection, some work, a bit of luck. He carefully removes her picture and résumé from the black portfolio, hands it to her, and takes out his own. They read them over, checking to see that all is in order; some light talk, back and forth. Then, after a moment of silence, except for the sound of a telephone ringing in the distance, he says to her, "Just don't use any of my minute or I'll leap across the room and bite you!"

Their names are called and they are ushered into an office. The door is shut. Exactly five minutes later, the door opens and they emerge, visibly unchanged, and walk down the hallway to the elevators.

Commercials are, in this country, one way an actor has to make the system support him, so that he is free to do the kind of work he wants to do. Many actors go through a period when they think that doing commercials is selling out, prostituting their artist soul. But they usually find themselves broke and add some realism to their idealism. An actress I know is trying to get her own theatre started in Los Angeles, but she is desperately in need of funds. She has been offered several decent commercials yet is hesitant about doing them. My feeling is that she is missing a connection here. If commercials are dangerous for an actor, it will be because they are really vulgar and unimaginative, or will somehow irrevocably connect an actor with a certain product in people's minds, turn them off, blind them, and pigeonhole the actor for a long time. If you spend a day in front of a television set, I think it is fairly easy to decide which commercials you would do, and which ones make you queasy. Try it (women especially, because although women appear in fewer commercials than men, they also seem to appear in more vulgar commercials than men).

Most actors I talked with who have done commercials are very selective about the ones they do. They will not endorse a product unless they use it or believe in it, and they prefer commercials that are character bits in which they appear as anonymous actors. They treat them like a job, an exercise in discipline and control, and do them for the money. One actor thinks of them as children's theatre: "The first commercial I did was one of the worst experiences in my life. I played an old trapper, and it took all day to shoot and it almost drove me mad. I remember, when we finally finished it, screaming, 'You can take your whatever and shove it!' I didn't realize what was wrong until later. I acted it, you see, and an actor is what I am. But commercials are not that—they are children's theatre, and you do not act them, you perform them, up front. I did two more after that. I went in and I just performed them, and that did the trick for me. It was my key, and it was what they wanted."

Commercials can be your bread and butter, and they can also mean exposure. Casting people and agents look at television. One actress reports, "A few years ago I did a deodorant commercial. They were just beginning to do those natural commercials. I wore my glasses and an old jean shirt and very little make-up, and I talked directly into the camera. That commercial was so successful that I had people calling me up to interview me for jobs. If a commercial is really good, it can be a showcase for an actor."

In the pursuit of income within the business, the field of commercials seems to gape like an open mouth. But it is a mouth full of teeth for those naïve or innocent or gullible enough to be seduced by certain ads which appear in the papers calling for "New Faces," or proclaiming "Success in TV Commercials Now!" I once answered an ad in a trade paper which read: "Faces for commercials—all types—unusual." I immediately decided that I must have an unusual face, and my overweening sense of specialness was fuel enough to get me to that office for an appointment. I met with a casting director who sat behind a desk in an office whose walls were covered with pictures cut out of magazines of naked girls riding motorcycles. The gentleman asked me if I could drive a motorcycle, play tennis, or ride a horse. And he told me that I had a good voice that would be great in voice-overs. But, he said, "We must first make a video tape of you, which will cost you fifty dollars." He would then decide from the tape whether he would "register" me with their company. If so, I would have to pay them another $200. For what? To sit in their files? "This ad must be for suckers," I told him. And he didn't argue.

In the trades from time to time, there are ads (or such and such management company seeking new faces) with claims that they will get your career started *at a low cost*. Avoid them like the plague! All they want is your money, and although they might claim that they will send your picture to agents, producers, and casting directors, they have no slick inroad to these people. They cannot do anything for your career that you can't do yourself directly.

One casting director who works in an advertising agency told me the way in which he selects actors for his commercials, and his remarks will be useful for anyone working in the field:

> I receive hundreds of pictures and résumés every month and on the basis of these will invite people to come in for

general interviews, which are of necessity very brief. I try my hardest to see everyone who wants to be seen, and in fact I think I do manage to do it.

If an actor arouses my interest or curiosity in an interview, I will eventually call him back for an audition —this call-back might happen in a month, or six months. It all depends on how busy we are. The audition requires the actor to bring in a five-minute scene of his choice. I always emphasize that the actor should choose a part that is close to him, something that he is likely to be cast in, and something that he can do well. I always prefer contemporary material—no Shakespeare, please—and I also prefer to see a scene with a partner, rather than a monologue. These auditions are held in a large room here, on a stage, and they are not videotaped.

Then, if I like the actor's work and a specific job comes up which I think he'd be right for, I call him back for a second audition. This time he will get a script of the commercial, and a storyboard to look at. The storyboard is a cartoon illustration of how the commercial will be shot, and what each cut will be. Some actors find this very helpful; others don't use them at all. It's up to them.

I have always preferred actors to nonactors for commercials, because I feel they are a better investment in the long run. They approach their work in a different way, and are presumably developing and growing in their craft, and are not content to remain the woman who sells detergent on TV.

Commercials are really tough to make, tougher than most young, inexperienced actors seem to realize, and they will often make the mistake of telling me in an interview that they want to do a commercial "just for the money." I realize, of course, that they are not intentionally demeaning commercials, but they do not realize how difficult they are to make, and they should not be the first job you try to get when you come to New York, wet behind the ears. Young actors don't realize that a commercial has to "happen" in fifty-eight, or sometimes thirty seconds.

HOW TO FIND WORK

3

In your pursuit of acting jobs, before you have an agent working for you (and even afterward), there are several ways to be your own agent, which is essentially putting yourself in the path of those people who can hire you or get you hired, making yourself visible and known to them.

MAKING ROUNDS

The process of making rounds is largely a New York City tradition, because actors there can still pound the pavement, knock on doors, leave their pictures and résumés in the offices of agents and casting directors, without being sent by an agent, as is the case in Hollywood. Admittedly, the business in the city is not as casual and open as it was in the 1960s. There is a little more red tape to cut your way through, more receptionists and outer-office screening, more locked doors (literally and probably just as much because of crime as well as a much larger population of unemployed actors seeking work). But, as one optimistic actor put it, "You can walk into an office tomorrow and get cast if you are determined enough."

Here is an actress's description of how she spent a month making rounds:

I took a month off from my job and went around the city every day making rounds. I bought myself a special outfit and rode my bike. I would get up every morning and dress and be out the door by eleven a.m. I had a book that lists every Equity, SAG, [Screen Actors Guild] and AFTRA [American Federation of Television and Radio Artists] agent, my folder of pictures and résumés, and a geographical breakdown of the city. I must have hit every agent and casting director in New York. I kept a record of what agents I went to, the impression I got from the office, and what was said to me, if anything. A couple of days later I would call and ask for an appointment. Sometimes I was told they weren't seeing anyone at that time. But I did get several interviews as a result of all my bike riding. Unfortunately, they were largely inconsequential. I would be told that I looked like a good commercial type, and that they would send my picture around, but nothing ever came of it.

Most actors don't enjoy this part of the business. "I don't like to make rounds. I find it the most depressing, degrading thing an actor has to do. When I go into agents' offices, I always seem to be confronted by the cold stares of snotty receptionists." But some actors seem to be able to make an art of it, and make this process work for them. I have a friend who makes the rounds all the time. He knows every casting director and agent in the city. He's all over the place. He walks into those offices and says, "Hi! I'm here!" He brings flowers to the secretaries and they all know him by name. It is a big business with him. He makes the rounds a lot and he works a lot. That's called hustling.

Making the rounds is your self-appointed work and it should be done on a regular or routine basis—and thoroughly. If you can't remember what an agent or casting director tells you when you drop by the office, write it down and keep a card-file system so that you will be able to follow through with telephone calls later. Be organized about it.

This part of your job really is not much fun. Think of it as work. It's your business. It's a way of making contacts. You are probably going to have to develop a rather detached, impersonal attitude or approach to it—surround your ego with some sort of invisible shield—to be able to endure it. You will definitely have to learn not to take the curt replies, annoyed looks, and the "noes" personally. And it will certainly be a test of your own will and drive and determination, for it is during this phase of making rounds that many actors throw in the towel: "I kept making rounds like crazy until one day it dawned on me that I could be doing it for the rest of my life and get absolutely nowhere because I had to fit into someone else's idea of who I was, which had nothing to do with who I really am."

One actor told a friend of his that he felt depressed because the full-time job he had made it difficult for him to make the rounds. His friend replied, "Listen, don't worry. Half the casting in this city is done at night at Joe Allen's or Jimmy Ray's [New York bars that are largely patronized by actors]."

That might be an exaggeration, but it is true that bars, parties, and openings are all places where the actors "grapevine" operates, where those elusive but all-important connections can be made, where you can hear about what's happening. If you sit in your apartment, you are not going to get a job. But these bars have a built-in danger as well. There is something comforting about being in a dark, smoke-filled bar with a lot of your fellow out-of-work actors all talking about hopes and dreams, about how good they are, and how great they will be once they get the chance. This can be as depressing as it is comfortable if the bar becomes a substitute for the real world.

TRADE PAPERS AND BULLETIN BOARDS

The other way you will function as your own agent is by faithfully reading the trades every week: *Back Stage, Show Business,* and *Variety* in New York (on the newsstands every Thursday); *Hollywood Reporter, Back Stage West,* and *Variety* in Hollywood. These trade papers will be your main source of casting information, although in Los Angeles the most up-to-date news is "published" by the grapevine and usually only the agents have the most recent inside line to what's happening.

Another source of information is bulletin boards: at the union offices, at your acting school, at the Drama Book Shop in New York, and the Theatre Communications Guild in New York. You can give them the once over as you make your rounds for casting notices and other information. It is important that you keep your finger on the networks of communication.

You will also find useful information about the location of various casting areas and theatres in the *Geographical Casting Guide for New York City Performers* (published four times a year by Lagos Enterprises, P.O. Box 149, Radio City, New York, N.Y. 10020, and available at the Drama Book Shop).

As soon as you have checked all your sources, circle casting calls in the papers or keep notes in a special booklet, in which you can also keep track of who has said what to you. Equipped with this information, you can then set out on your rounds. But first, you will need some material to help you sell yourself to the people with the jobs: a folder of pictures and résumés, and perhaps some other portfolio items, depending on what kind of job you are seeking.

BASIC EQUIPMENT

Q. How important do you think pictures are?
A. You just gotta have them!
Q. What if you don't have a résumé?
A. Make one up!

Buck Henry—Actor

We were all broke, we all lived on unemployment insurance when we could get it. We stole from the A & P and drank ten-cent glasses of beer, and wasted a fortune on those fucking pictures, on those pathetic composites which are filed in every convenient wastebasket, but which you have to have because it proves that you are who you say you are. All I know is that I must have laid out a thousand pictures and résumés and composites and I don't think any one ever did me any good—ever. And why should it? It was just another picture of a twenty-something-year-old average-looking guy with a few uninteresting credits.

William S. Miles—Actor

In my day the résumé had not been heard of. Now, apparently, it is your passport to heaven, a beautifully printed résumé with glossy photographs of you in unfamiliar poses. Without them, you can't get past the office boy.

Photographs

Everything about my desire to be an actress was hard for me except my dreams of fame and glory which came easy. At acting school I watched the other students come and go, always prepared with their pictures and résumés stashed under their arms. But I had an incredibly naïve attitude about myself and about the business. It wasn't a business—it was art and romance. Looking for the hard way out, I thought for some reason that I was different, that I wouldn't have to arm myself with those two ancillary items, or play the game the conventional way. I did it my way. I went to open calls thinking that if They would just see me and let me read, that would be enough. That would be It. Instant discovery. Each time I appeared at a call and was asked, "Your picture and résumé, please," I would say: "Well, I'm having new pictures printed up"; or "I just mailed my last one out, but will send you one tomorrow." The result was that I managed to get seen and read a few lines once or twice. Otherwise I was told, Sorry—I couldn't be seen without them. I was the basketball player that shows up at the game without his sneakers.

So I gave in. All right, I told myself, if I need these things to get to see the people in control, and if they are flooded with hundreds of eight-by-ten glossies of face after face after face, eyeballing them in black and white, then my picture had just better be different. A show-stopper.

It was. After spending a damp day on the Bowery with a photographer friend and an amiable bum who liked his Thunderbird slightly chilled and also liked to ham it up, I had my picture. The bum and me. The result was contrived and pretentious—a bedraggled girl with a vague look in her eye and her mouth slightly ajar, coupled with a weather-beaten old man, a far more interesting character. The picture was confusing and unclear and a dead giveaway—amateur was written across my forehead.

The eight-by-ten glossy head shot is a requirement of the business. It will often be the only way you have to bring yourself to the attention of a potential employer, get you in the door to get the job. You will present them at open calls, mail them out to agents, casting directors, directors, producers, for future auditions or interviews. It's your first line of attack, your first step in introducing yourself to the people on the other side of the desk.

There is no reason why you can't have a picture that will work to your advantage. It is important to remember that you are in a business that requires you to sell your Self. You are your own product—and the market is flooded. So you must not be vague or hesitant about what it is you are selling and why it is unique, interesting, different.

Experiment. If you have a friend who is a photographer it might be easier to get the result you want. You will have the freedom to fool around and be relaxed about the photographing session. Spend a day shooting outdoors, indoors, and have fun with it.

If not, talk to other actors whose pictures you like. Investigate commercial photographers who advertise in the trade papers. Visit several studios, look at their work, talk with the photographer and find out how comfortable he makes you feel, how relaxed you can be with him. And, of course, find out exactly what you will get for your money.

A lot of young actors feel they have to spend a fortune on pictures for their portfolio, pictures showing them in every guise imaginable. And many commercial photographers will try to convince an actor that he needs a huge array of pictures illustrating his different "looks." Well, that's their business, but in my opinion it's a waste of time and money.

Basically, what you will need are two good head shots—eight-by-ten glossies on a light background—featuring two different expressions.* Most photographers will take from sixty to eighty shots in a session and print them up on a contact sheet from which you can choose the ones you like. When you get this contact sheet, take a poll among your friends *and* enemies. Get their opinions on the shots they like and weigh them against your preferences and the photographer's preference, and then make your decision. The photographer's fee should include the purchase of two negatives from the sheet, and it can be as cheap as $25.

Your next step will be to have these pictures mass-duplicated. There are services that specialize in this and advertise their prices in the trades. The prices run from 13¢ to 15¢ a copy.

Leo Garen, a director who has done casting for both theatre and film talked to me about actors' pictures:

Agents, particularly the ones in California, are always telling actors to get very conventional-looking photographs. And there are certain photographers who make a living just doing actors' portfolios, again and again. They are usually studio-shot things and are almost indistinguishable. If you are in the middle of casting something, you come in in the morning and there are five hundred envelopes on your desk. Somebody has to open them and stack them—men here, women over there, and so forth.

* Some actors have composites made up (anywhere from three to seven shots arranged on an eight-by-ten photograph, showing them in various make-ups and poses) which I think tend to look hokey and contrived. Its over-all effect is unclear, confusing, and the impact of a good eight-by-ten head shot is diluted.

You start by going through them and looking quickly at the picture and résumé. Here is something that actors should remember: get a picture that looks like you! A million times you see a photograph of an extremely beautiful nineteen-year-old girl and when you call her in, she's twenty-nine and not quite that pretty. And you happened to have called her because you need a very pretty girl for the part. It is not just a question of age and physical attractiveness. Get a picture that looks like you! Get a photograph that, without being ornate and fancy, at least has some freshness and originality and simplicity to it. I can't tell you how many times I've gone through photographs and I'm stopped by one—one out of every hundred. And I say, "Hmmm, that's interesting." And I think, Well, if this actor has had the imagination and taste to come up with this picture, I'll see him.

Keep in mind the fact that although a picture won't get you a job, it just might get you in the door to get the job.

Résumés

Now that you have your picture, turn it over. Carefully stapled to the back of your eight-by-ten glossy will be your résumé. Getting a résumé together is a lot easier than getting a good picture, and you'll need one, in one form or another, just as you will need those pictures. They go together, although they often seem more symbolic than functional or helpful. They are part of the rules of the game and, up to a certain point, you have to follow the rules.

If you have no résumé at all, outside of a production of *As You Like It* in high school, you have two alternatives: you can tell the truth or you can concoct a feasible résumé of parts in plays that you *could* have done, that are representative of you, that are close to you as a type. If you are nineteen years old, it is not going to help you much to say that you played an eighty-year-old deaf mute in some play, even if it's true.

The whole point of these theatrical autobiographies is that unless you can truthfully say that you had a part in a play or movie that the people on the other side of the desk are going to know about or have heard about, your high-school productions or your white lies about plays and student films aren't going to matter much to anyone.

To lie or not to lie? that is the question. And the answer is a tossup. One Hollywood producer gives this advice:

> My advice to beginning actors is to lie. That's the prime thing that they have to do. They have to lie about their backgrounds because the actor has to get the job first. It's no good if you can't get the job and the reason that starting actors can't get jobs is because people who hire actors are afraid that they won't be able to perform professionally.

A casting director I talked to thinks it is silly to lie, and that it's hard to do so effectively without getting caught. But another director told me:

> Make it up! Make up college productions, et cetera, et cetera. Everybody knows that three fourths of what you read in résumés are lies, or inflated. Just don't put anything down that you are going to be embarrassed about being caught at. Lie with finesse and with taste. Of course, the other approach is to write a paragraph which is the absolute truth: "I've been in New York for a year. I acted in high school and college. I've studied with so and

so and am now studying with so and so. I was in a three-minute film. Please see me."

Then, I remember, he threw up his hands and shrugged.

How to Prepare a Résumé
This is the information that should appear on your résumé:

Name:
Height:
Weight:
Hair color:
Eye color:
Age range:
Telephone number and service number:
Agent's number:
Your credits in order of their importance (professional credits should come first; if you have been in any radio or television commercials, list them by name):
Training (acting, singing, dance; whom you study with):
Special talents (knowledge of foreign languages or special performing skills):
Union affiliations:

Your résumé should be neat, clean, accurately typed, and easy to read. If you happen to have done a hundred plays in high school and college, don't feel that it will be impressive to list them all. Be selective. A one-page résumé is all that anyone will take the time to read, assuming they read it all.

Reviews
Save your good reviews and not just for your scrapbook. Make them an integral part of your portfolio, and have Xeroxed copies made of them that you can mail out with your picture and résumé. It can be embarrassing or

awkward to tout your own talent, so let the reviews do it for you. For some reason, people have a genuine respect for print; if they can see it in black and white, they'll believe it, and your credibility will be enhanced.

Postcards

Most photography-lab services which specialize in reproducing high-gloss photographs and reprinting résumés will also make up photo postcards—standard-size postcards featuring your picture, name, and telephone number. The minimum standard order is two hundred and prices are usually reasonable. These cards can be useful to have on hand and will save you the expense of giving away your eight-by-ten glossies when you wish to remind an agent or casting director that you are alive and well and looking for work. They can also serve as a way of inviting crucial people to a production in which you have a good-size part; simply attach one to the flier announcing the play, with a note saying that you would very much like so-and-so to attend and that you will reserve seats if he or she wishes. They are a good means of keeping in touch, of saying "remember me."

Tapes, Video and Audio

Both of these items are fairly expensive to have made, and made well, and it is seldom that you will be *required* to have either. But an excellent voice-over tape or a beautiful video tape could serve to your advantage, especially for work in the field of television commercials, television movies, and films. They will give some added depth to a ten-minute interview with a casting agent.

If you are interested, you might investigate the services that specialize in making voice-over tapes and videotapes for commercials and auditions; these are advertised in the trade papers. Better yet, get a recommendation from someone you trust and who is familiar with the problems involved, and follow his suggestions as to the right music, the right copy, and good direction.

Answering Service

An answering service is easy to get and important to have. It will be your hot line to the outside world, and act as your secretary when you are out pounding the pavement. The telephone is an incredibly important means of communication in this business, and it is essential for you that "someone" is always home.

There are several different kinds of services you can get, depending on how much money you have to spend:

1. Most actors use an answering service that takes messages for them at a special telephone number. This type of service can be very cheap—less than $10 a month for twenty-four-hour-a-day service. And if it is a reliable company, that service is quite adequate. It is up to you to check in with them regularly, to get your messages.

2. A variation on this is the kind of answering service that will pick up your phone when you are not at home and take messages. This one costs quite a bit more.

3. If you have some money to invest, you can buy your own answering service—a gadget that is attached to your phone, and that will answer your calls with a recording and then tape all messages. Cost: $60–100.

The answering services that cater to actors advertise in the trade papers, and there are more in the Yellow Pages. Once you get one and get things rolling, keep in touch with them. How often you call them every day is up to you. One actor I spoke with told me that he calls in every few hours, in between making rounds and doing his nonacting jobs which pay his rent: "Heaven forbid that I should miss a call because I didn't check with my service that hour!"

TRYING OUT

4

There is an art to auditioning and my agent said you know I have people who have minimal talent but they get the jobs all the time because they audition well. Most of the actors I know who are really gifted are just not that great in auditions.

—ACTRESS

If I were walking into a producer's office for an interview, I would much rather be seen carrying something more interesting than Variety *or* Hollywood Reporter *since people do not notice that kind of thing. I inevitably ask an actor what he's reading, partly because I'm curious and partly because it's something to talk about.*

—CASTING DIRECTOR

INTERVIEWS

The interview is usually the first step in a long elimination process that you will go through to get cast in a part. It is a preliminary meeting between you, the actor, and the producer and/or director and/or casting director, who for reasons of time and money, is trying to see as many people as possible in the shortest length of time. This is how one director explained this process to me:

> Actors who find themselves sitting in waiting rooms and walking in and saying a few sentences to the guy on the other side of the desk and being told "Thank you very much" always feel that they have been put through this terrible procedure. But, in point of fact, what is usually going on is that there are five or ten roles that you want to cast. You have a notion of what you are after. Someone comes in and you talk with them, and after you have done this a thousand times you begin to feel, rightly or wrongly, that there are certain personal ways you have of assessing, at least on a superficial level, the actors you are meeting—whether it is their physical appearance, or the way they sound, the way they respond, their experience, or just a sense you get of them, whether they are in any way in the direction of what you are looking for.

It is important to keep in mind the idea that these people on the other side of the desk are not engaged in some kind of conspiracy to keep you from getting the part, and that they are looking for the right person just as hard as you are looking for a job.

It can't be helped that these interviews are by nature subjective and superficial, that you will feel a great amount of pressure to "do something" to show them who you really are, how good and wonderful you are, and that you will continually be frustrated by their snap judgments: too tall, too short, too fat, too thin, too ethnic, too Wasp, too young, too old, or too inexperienced. There are not many people in the business who are willing to take risks and give you the chance to prove yourself. I once got down to the wire for a big part in a play and was finally rejected because, as the director explained to me, I hadn't done a full-length play and she was afraid that I wouldn't be able to carry it. She was afraid, and I was furious, but the power in that case—as it often is when an actor is seeking and not being sought—was in her hands and that was that.

Many anxious actors feel compelled to "come on" in one way or another because of the pressure inherent in the interview situation. One actor says: "It's amazing what characters emerge from you when you're being interviewed. It's so strange, as if a whole other person takes over and starts being really interesting. And that person is never as interesting as you really are." Some will come on effusive and pushy, saying corny things: "I've wanted to meet you more than anyone else in the whole world," which usually makes interviewers shrivel up and lose interest. Or an actor will come on hostile and defiant, which can be the way one actually feels in a confrontation of this kind if one assumes that the guys on the other side of the desk are out to get you and are trying *not* to give you a part. That hostility will not only tie an actor up in knots but it will also make things very uncomfortable for the director or producer, and he will probably write that actor off very quickly.

An actor may fall into being wildly funny just out of nervousness or smile broadly for moments on end. This approach is just as uninteresting as the hostile one—a grin from ear to ear is as transparent as Jell-O. I was once embarrassed but greatly relieved when a director told me with some emphasis, "Wipe that smile off your face." Another ineffectual approach is to come on demanding or desperate. The people who are casting don't want to be shouted at or argued with, and they don't want to hear how hard up an actor is.

Some actors in an anything-goes state of mind will try shock tactics with the idea that they will get attention and be remembered. One casting director pointed out to me: "Women will often come into an interview dressed in the most incredibly sexy clothes, sexier than what they usually wear. And it will be obvious that they have gone to a lot of trouble. It is going to get them some attention, but what happens is that you wind up never really looking at the actress. You wind up looking at her body. And I think there is something destructive and distasteful about it." As to the use of flirting: "The flirting stuff usually backfires because there is more than one man in the room and either the actress is going to flirt with the wrong guy or she's going to flirt with the right guy but he won't respond because the others know what she's doing."

Which brings up the question of the casting-couch approach. I think it is very naïve for an actress to think that if she sleeps with someone, a kind of bartering—the sex for the part—is going to take place. Obviously, it has worked for some, and I'm sure many producers have given actresses small parts in movies for their services, but the chances of that kind of exchange taking place are not very good. Sex is a pretty cheap commodity when it gets to the casting-couch level, and the men in theatre and films who are serious about their work, whether it be producing, directing, agenting or whatever—and women, too, of course—are not in business to be doing favors, especially when their money, egos, and reputations are at stake. Don't be a dupe. This kind of compromise will hurt you more in the long run and it certainly won't make you a more talented actor. As one actress put it, "I have slept with every man who I thought might be in a position to help me get my big break. I have flirted, played coy, necked with, stripped for, whatever, to make connections. I thought it was part of the game, part of the whole business—but it has never gotten me a part. And I know why. It's because I'm a bad actress, and I should face up to that fact and do something else."

That the casting couch is still a reality is confirmed by an article which appeared in *Variety* in May 1975. According to the article, the Screen Actors Guild is currently trying to figure out a way to set up a bureau designated to investigate complaints of a moral nature made by its members. It seems that there has been an increase in the number of complaints made by the union's members—complaints involving producers and directors *and* union members as well. We'll see what happens.

Some actors will choose attention-getting devices that are rather more subtle than blatantly sexual. One casting director recalls "a very talented actor who came in, took out an orange, and proceeded to peel that orange and eat it while we talked. He was doing that to get attention, and you could say that he succeeded because I remember it, but I don't remember it with a good feeling. If anything, I found it to be pretentious." It is understandable that an actor feels he has to pull some stunt to be noticed, especially if he is number 324 on a list and has five minutes to appeal. But I polled a lot of people on the other side of the desk as to how effective these kinds of tactics really were, and the results were pretty unanimously negative. Granted that some sort of eccentric behavior has resulted in an actor getting a shot at a part he might not have gotten had he behaved normally, and granted that it has sometimes gotten an actor the part—with regrets later all around. But, in general, what an actor chooses to do to shock is most always something that has been done before, and it is unappreciated, it is an insult to the intelligence of the director or producer or casting director, and an insult to the actor's intelligence. The impression left is a bad one, and the actor is remembered for the stupid or silly thing he did.

A movie director I spoke with tells a bit of what it's like on the other side of the desk:

On my last film, I saw actors for four months at fifteen-minute intervals, all day. And you gradually go blind. Actors pass through the room without your really seeing them. I've tried all the different ways of saying no. I've tried saying, "No, you're not right for this. I have something else in mind." I've tried saying, "Thank you very much, that's very good. We'll be in touch." And what I finally found myself doing is the last one. With any other response you'll find that actors will yell back at you. If you say, "You're really not what I have in mind," they'll say, "Well, give me a chance!" And you don't like them, you don't think they are any good, and you want to get them out of the office as fast as you can without being yelled at. Whatever you do, a certain percentage of actors are going to yell back because they are nervous and they realize that they haven't got the part, and they have nothing to lose. And I have cast people who have yelled at me because I have been struck by their yelling. I've regretted it later though, because the yelling continued. So you find yourself doing the thing that will make the least amount of waves, which is to give them a little cruel hope. And actors will go to great lengths to attract your attention if they realize that you are not really seeing them. They behave in kooky ways or they take their clothes off. But I've seen all those, so it doesn't do any good. The actor I eventually cast came in and read extremely well. Somebody can come in and be so blindingly good that they get through the haze that forms in front of your eyes.

Hints for an Interview

Although there is no science to the interview and there is no cure for nervousness, there are certain things that an actor can do that will make the interview less of an ordeal, less intimidating, more human, and more interesting:

1. Find out as much as you can about the people you are going to meet. You should have the kind of background on them that you wish they had on you—and deal with them as people.

2. Find out as much as you can about the part you are going up for. Ask your agent. Try to read the script or the play.

3. Wear clothes that make you feel good, look great, and that you are comfortable in. When you are going up for a part, whether it is an interview, a reading, or an audition, use your judgment about the clothes you wear. Ask the producer or casting director if he would like you to wear anything in particular when you are called back to read. Most obviously, don't dress in a way that is going to hurt your interview. Don't presume that the casting people are going to be able to imagine you one way if you appear another. Don't make them do all the work to see you as a certain type of character. It is ridiculous to dress as a farm girl if that is the part you are up for. But it is equally ridiculous to come dressed up in high heels and red lips and a tight black dress. Certainly, if you are being seriously considered for the part of a teen-ager and get called back for a third reading, don't suddenly appear looking like a twenty-five-year-old sophisticate. That will throw everyone off and will probably be fatal. One director recalls, "An

actress came in for a part in a picture I was casting. She was very tough and aggressive and had short, short hair. We talked and she said, 'You know, I love this part; I've never played a lesbian before.' I asked her what she was talking about, there was no lesbian in this picture. She said, 'Oh my god, I've done it all wrong!' and she took off the wig she was wearing. Underneath it she had long, flowing hair, and suddenly she was quite beautiful. Her whole manner had changed."

4. Be on time for your appointment. Bring your picture and résumé with you, and your portfolio if you have one.

5. In an interview, you will have a very important job to do: be yourself. Be who you are, actively and specifically. It sounds simple—there are no lines to learn—but it is deceptive. Actors dislike interviews because they feel they cannot be themselves. Instead, they flounder around, trying every which way to be "something," and trying to read the minds of the casting people; but this will never work. You are not going to get inside their heads and find out what they are looking for, and if you could you would probably discover, seven times out of ten, that they aren't sure themselves. Don't try to anticipate who it is they want to walk through the door, for you will be wrong. Assume and believe that they want *you* to walk through the door. And do it. Knowing who you are, and being able to be that person is the key to the whole shebang. It will take a lot of work and practice, but these interviews are going to be important for you.

6. Don't overstay your welcome. Don't try to stretch out the interview. Have sense enough to know when it is finished, and leave. Believe it or not, actors have ruined their chances for a part by staying too long at the ball.

COLD READINGS

The cold reading is a method used by casting people to sift the wheat from the chaff, and it's a method that is largely unappreciated by actors. The usual procedure is to hand the actor three pages or so of script, tell him to go outside and look it over, and then come back in and read it. No sensible director or producer expects the actor to come in and give anything resembling a performance in that kind of circumstance. What they are interested in doing is getting a sense of the actor in relationship to a certain part, some smell of how the actor and the role fit together. In a cold reading they learn things about an actor: how inventive he is, how well he reads, how well he listens, and whether he really talks to the person he is reading with. And sometimes they are very surprised by what an actor will do, seeing things in the part they didn't see before.

A cold reading will often be the second phase of your interview with the director, producer, or casting director. But just as often it will be the first meeting you have with him. After you have handed in your picture with the résumé on the back to a receptionist, you may be given a script to read over while you wait—in an office or hallway, or on a staircase with your fellow actors and your competition—for your number to come up.

One actor has this to say about cold readings: "I don't like them because casting people are always looking for immediate results—some big emotion—and so I always feel I have to push for that. I used to go to readings and just read very simply and I never got called back for anything. Then I started pushing for results and I landed a couple of parts. But now I find myself working for a combination of the two—and I think I know more about what it means to be 'simple.' It doesn't mean being low-keyed or monotonous or without energy."

The conditions under which most readings are held are not ones that make the process easy for an actor. More often they seem deliberately set up to make life as hard as possible for you. It would be wonderful if casting people mimeographed hundreds of scripts and gave them ahead of time to everyone they are interested in for a part, letting him take some time to prepare a scene. But time and money won't allow this kind of indulgence because, as one director points out, "the speed in which you want to cast something, or the limited amount of time you have in that city, or because you have to see nine hundred more actors that day, you want to get a feeling about the actor then and there."

In the best of circumstances, an actor will be given some information about the character and the story, either by the director or in a summary of the script.* In the worst of circumstances, you won't be told anything at all, and you will find yourself sitting in a fly-by-night office, with your "judges" practically sitting in your lap, reading with a secretary or assistant, and after about three minutes you will be stopped and told: 'Thank you very much. We'll be in touch.' "

Being able to cold read effectively is not necessarily an indication of talent and many actors have been mistakenly called back or cast in an unsuitable role on the basis of good cold readings. But it is certainly to your advantage to be able to do it well, even if your presentation is slick. If you can display a certain amount of skill and experience, those

---

* The reading will take place on a stage or in a large room, often with another actor. A thoughtful director will try to make you feel relaxed and help you as much as possible.

who are looking you over will have some confidence in you as a professional.

Hints for Cold Reading

There is no right way to learn how to cold read, because it is not a science, but here are some ways to approach it:

1. Practice. Practice at home. Practice with a tape recorder. Practice with other actors in class. And practice by going to try for as many parts as you can, where you will have real pressures and a real case of nerves. Think of these tryouts as free classes.

2. When you are handed a scene and have ten minutes to read it over, don't panic and don't try to do too much. If something interesting occurs to you, a character element or a simple gesture, try it, even if it seems arbitrary; use that element as a focus for your reading and carry it through. Let the director know that you have an idea about the character, even if it may not be the same idea he has.

3. If you have a chance, ask if there is anything particular they would like you to work on. You might be asked to do the impossible. Don't argue. Take a moment and try to do it anyway.

I was once asked to do an imitation of Mick Jagger singing "You Can't Always Get What You Want", and this was pretty much how everyone felt after it was over. But you have to remember that if they have any brains at all, they are not expecting an exciting, polished performance—although that is not always the case.

4. Take your time. Don't feel you have to race through the scene to get it over with. Take time to listen to the other actor (or secretary) and deal with him personally.

5. Don't glue yourself to the words in the script or to your seat.

6. Read simply and naturally in your own style and don't push for a result that you think the director wants to see. As one casting director explains, "Some people are looking for results, but I am always looking for a kind of simple use of the personality."

7. Have fun. Don't make the reading into a life-and-death situation. It's a game.

If the director likes what you do in a cold reading, he will want to find out if you can do it again, or perhaps what else you can do. And this is when a lot of inexperienced actors flunk out. A director explains, "I've seen people give spectacular first readings, and I've gotten very excited and had them take a script home and come back the next day. And what I often find out is that what the actor did in a cold reading was a fortuitous accident that was simply the result of his tension."

On a call-back, you might be given the same scene to prepare, or you might be given a new scene to work on. And the director may give you some instructions, some aspect of the character to work on, or he may not tell you a thing, leaving it all in your hands. More will be expected of you the second time; you will at least be expected to be consistent, and probably better. The ball has been thrown into your court, and this is when you will have the opportunity to demonstrate your craft.

SCREEN TESTS

In her autobiography Frances Farmer describes her first screen test for Paramount Pictures in 1935:

I reported to the makeup department, where Eddie Senz was assigned to prepare me. I was in his chair for hours, during which time my hair was hacked off and my eyebrows shaved off. I was furious and ready to walk out, but they kept telling me that I would be happy with the finished product. Finally I was curled and powdered to their satisfaction, and they allowed me to look at myself in the mirror.

A strange, sleek creature stared back at me and I was horrified. Nothing was left of Frances Farmer, and I exploded. Warned that nobody except Mr. Serlin* "threw a shoe" when he was around, I quieted down and went through the test, doing a good job. When it was finished, I looked at Mr. Serlin questioningly. He left the studio with a single curt comment; "We'll let you know."

Angrily I scrubbed my face until it was raw, and I burst into tears when I saw the wide, hairless span above my eyes. . . . The whole impersonal business grated on me. "They'll not make a goddamned wampus baby out of me," I stormed.

Shelley Duval describes a rather different sort of screen test—the one she took for a role in *Brewster McCloud*: "Bud Cort came to town and we did a screen test together. It was done in a rose garden in Houston, and it was all improvisation. I was hanging on to a statue of a Greek man with wings and talking, talking about myself. A couple of days later, we started shooting the picture."

Regardless of the various demands put on an actor, the purpose of the screen test is obvious—to see how an actor looks on film. Something happens when an actor's appearance is translated through the medium of film onto the screen. It has been called mysterious, magical, indescrib-

* New York talent chief for Paramount Pictures.

able; but whatever it is, something happens. The image an actor projects in the flesh can be totally different when it is magnified, as if through a giant microscope, on the screen. The image might be enhanced—or it might, somehow, be lost.

Although the screen test is not used as routinely as it was during the Golden Age of Hollywood, and many actors are cast in films without one, you are likely to be tested if you are down to the wire with other actors competing for the same part and if you don't have any film in your portfolio to show. The results of this screen test can be crucial to your career. Andrea Eastman told me that when she was casting for Paramount Pictures in the late 1960s, she was looking for new faces. When Paramount decided to find a brand-new girl for *Goodbye, Columbus*, they called in a lot of beautiful New York models, hoping that one of them could act. They selected seven of them to screen-test, and although Ali MacGraw had been called in, she was not one of the seven they chose. Apparently, none of the seven passed the test, because they recalled Ali, tested her, and she got the part.

There is no routine screen test. A lot will depend on the producer or director, and on the budget of the picture. The test might be done very casually, and you might be asked to improvise. You could be given a script and asked to learn a scene which you will do in street clothes standing in front of the camera. Or the test can be an elaborate affair shot in a studio with makeup and costumes. Sometimes a test will be done just to see how you look with another actor who has already been cast for the film.

Seeing yourself on film for the first time is very much like hearing your voice on tape for the first time—it is a shock. You see yourself as a stranger but from a frighteningly intimate perspective. The intimidation caused by the camera, the lights, and the crew can be crippling, freezing you up and turning you off. Obviously, the more experience you can get in front of a camera, the better prepared you will be.

There are commercial classes given in television and film acting which use videotape and closed-circuit television. Such classes tend to be expensive, but they might be a worthwhile investment if you have never worked in front of a camera before. Another way of getting experience is to become involved with film students and independent film-makers who are always looking for actors to work for free on their projects. They usually put casting notices in the trade papers, as well as on the bulletin boards at various acting schools. Even getting involved as a nonactor can have results. I once worked on a low-low-budget film as a combination script girl and go-fer, and wound up getting a part in the film.

PREPARED AUDITIONS

Many auditions, especially those for theatre, will require that you present a selection of prepared work. You will be asked to bring in two contrasting pieces—one classic and one contemporary, or one comic and one serious—usually not to exceed two or three minutes each. They can be monologues or short scenes with a partner, or a combination of these. A prepared audition is vastly preferable to a cold reading because rather than being faced with an unfamiliar scene from an unfamiliar script, you will have the opportunity to perform material of your own choosing which you have had the time to work on and perfect. You will be in command of those five minutes and will, in effect, be saying, "This is what I can do and can do well."

The selection of the material is of prime importance and

demands some know-how on your part: knowing how you come across as an actor and what qualities you project, knowing your own range and limitations, knowing yourself as a product that is for sale. You are the casting director and you are casting yourself. Avoid worn-out audition pieces which are so familiar that twenty other actors will use the same piece. As one theatre director puts it, "Please, I never want to hear another 'To be or not to be' or the Maid's speech from *The Skin of Our Teeth* or anything from *Antigone!*" Look for material that is original and fresh, but not obscure, and select a scene that will be self-contained.

Because of the time limit imposed upon you, you will probably have to cut the scene. This is sometimes difficult to do without losing some of the development and impact, but it can be done. Discover the core of the scene and throw out the rest. And don't make the mistake of thinking that you will be allowed to go over the time limit specified. You might be given an extra minute to finish, but more often than not you will be stopped with a "Lights up" and "Thank you very much." I once made this mistake in an audition, and when they stopped me all I could think was, But I haven't gotten to the good part yet! You have to get to the good part right away.

Most actors and casting people I have talked with seem to prefer scenes to monologues. Casting people find scenes more interesting and more indicative of the actor's talent, and actors feel more comfortable working with a partner, especially if it is someone he has worked with before. It will always be to your advantage if the actor you pick to work with is good; if your scene partner is a lousy actor, you will probably not look better because the scene itself will not come off well.

But if you don't have time to work up a scene with a

partner, don't try to do one alone. One director says that he "discourages" people from attempting to do a scene in which they play two or three parts alone, moving back and forth from one part to another. It's clever but diffused and their concentration is almost always on the technique of changing rather than on any one character. If you are to audition alone, do a monologue instead, and make sure that it *is* a monologue. Setting up an imaginary character on stage to address yourself to or using your auditioner to speak to will make you appear to be as green as a shamrock.

Don't encumber your audition with complicated changes of clothes, props, sound effects, or tapes. A carefully selected piece of clothing or a single prop can be just as effective and ingenious as an elaborate costume or stage set. Pick something that works for you, something that you can relate to and work with, and that helps you get into your scene as fast as possible.

Who Wants Prepared Scenes?

The following prospective employers are likely to ask for prepared scenes as part of the tryout process:

1. Summer stock companies.

2. Regional theatre and repertory companies.

3. TCG auditions.

4. Television casting directors regularly hold general auditions which usually require a five-minute contemporary scene.

5. Non-Equity plays (Off-Off-Broadway). Rather than have you cold-read, the director will often ask if you have a monologue that you can do for him.

6. Agents. If an agent is interested in you and has not seen you work, he might ask you to bring in a couple of scenes.

7. Casting directors, film directors.

The actor has two major responsibilities in the business of acting. The first is to be in the right place at the right time—an unwritten dictate with a lot of myth and mystery attached to it. Let's leave that one for the moment in the hands of the gods or fate or fashion.

And the second is to be prepared when he happens to land in the right place at the right time, which many actors tend to overlook, or to be lazy about. It is very easy to wait until someone is interested in you before you prepare yourself for a tryout, but when that happens it might be too late. One actress told me that she had been trying for weeks to get an interview with a certain agent. She finally got her appointment, and went in to talk to him. He asked her, after a five-minute chat, if she had a monologue she could do for him. "Now?" she said. "Yes, darling, right now," he answered. Needless to say, she didn't, and he dismissed her with a "Let me know when you're in something and I'll come and see it."

It's very important that you begin to look for scenes and monologues even before you start making rounds, that you read an hour every day with the prepared audition in mind, and that you build up a personal repertoire which you can call on at a moment's notice or can work up in a day or less. Otherwise, you will be caught empty-handed and find yourself rushing around frantically looking for a scene, looking for an actor to work with you, and coming up with an unsatisfying, slap-dash performance.

Get together seven to ten good scenes and monologues. These will be your bag of tricks. Nobody ultimately cares about your credits. What they want to know is: What can you show me now?

UNION MEMBERSHIP

5

You can't get a union job unless
you're in the union
And you can't get into the union
without a union job. . . .

And so on. Every actor sings this song because every actor has faced this Kafka-like dilemma at one point or another. It looms ahead like a brick wall that you will bang your head against at least once in your career. A glance through the casting section of *Show Business* or *Back Stage* or *Variety* tells you why—most of the casting notices call for Equity or SAG members only. And until you get a union job, you aren't going to be making any money in your profession.

Actors who haven't managed to get into a union resent the fact that the unions make it so difficult to join. Actors in the union resent the fact that there are so many members of the union competing for so few jobs. Some have even voiced the opinion that simply being hired for a union job should not be the only qualification to become a member of a union, and that potential members should be required to prove themselves before a committee by an audition or some sort of test of professionalism. But whatever side of the fence you happen to be on, there are always going to be too many actors applying for too few jobs (that seems to be one of the unwritten rules of the profession), and until you get into a union, your job opportunities and income are going to be limited.

Union Facts and Fees

Associated Actors and Artists of America (4A's) is the national organization under which six separate unions are gathered, including the three dramatic unions which will concern you: Actors Equity Association (AEA), Screen Actors Guild (SAG), and American Federation of Television and Radio Artists (AFTRA). (The other 4A unions are the American Guild of Musical Artists [AGMA], the American Guild of Variety Artists [AGVA], and the Screen Extras Guild [SEG].)

1. *Actors Equity Association* encompasses all professional performers in the legitimate theatre in the United States and Canada. This union's jurisdiction covers Broadway, Off-Broadway, touring companies, stock companies, café-theatres, repertory theatres, industrial shows, dinner theatres, and children's theatres. You become a member of Equity by signing an Equity contract, or through a reciprocal arrangement with the other 4A unions: if you are a paid-up member for *six months* of one of the other 4A unions, you are allowed to join Equity without an Equity contract. The current Equity fees include an initiation fee of $300 and a $21 minimum in dues payable twice a year. These dues are based on your earnings and will increase as your earnings increase. If you are a member of another union, you will be given a $150 credit toward the initiation fee.

2. *Screen Actors Guild* covers acting work in the motion-

picture field, including motion pictures for television, for theatres, filmed commercials, motion pictures for industrial and commercial uses, and for educational, religious, and other purposes (in other words, all acting work done on film). You become a member of SAG by signing a contract as a principal in a union film. Or, if you have been a paid-up member of one of the other 4A unions for *one year*, you are permitted to join SAG without a contract. The initiation fee for SAG is currently $300, plus a minimum of $20 in dues payable twice a year. As with Equity, if you are a member of another union, your initiation fee is reduced to $150, and the dues payable involve a minimum of $12.50 twice a year.

3. *American Federation of Television and Radio Artists* has jurisdiction over all live and videotaped television programs, radio and television commercials, radio programs, phonograph recordings, slide films, closed-circuit television, cable television, and others. AFTRA is an open union, which means that you can join without a contract simply by paying the initiation fee of $300, following up with dues of $27.50 every six months. AFTRA will also allow you to work in a job covered by its jurisdiction for thirty days *without* joining the union. For instance, you can do as many videotaped commercials as you can get for a period of thirty days before you have to come up with the money to join this union. There is talk that AFTRA will not remain an open union forever, but to this date it still is. (There is also talk of consolidating AFTRA and SAG into one union.)

Actors will always try to circumvent the restrictions of a union casting call until they get into the unions because it often seems to be the only way to get to see those people they have to see to get hired. They will fake a union card or borrow a union card to get into an open call. This practice is both illegal and risky, and you could be in some trouble if you are found out. Some people will lie about union affiliation on their résumés. A casting director at an advertising agency told me that a lot of actors do this, but she strongly advises against it. If she happens to cast you as an extra in a commercial, she will check you out with the union and should she discover that you are not a member, she's going to be angry, you're going to be embarrassed, and you might lose the job. Other actors will fight the restrictions. One actress I interviewed said that she once went to an Equity call ready to demand to be seen, despite the fact that she was not a member of the union. She was very surprised to find that time had been set aside for nonunion actors to try out for this particular production. "But in most cases," she said, "I do a lot of fast talking. It is a spur-of-the-moment thing, whatever I think will get to them. I either demand my rights or come on very friendly and very reasonable. It is like another acting job for me; my fighting for a chance to be seen gets me into more places than I'd get into if I just walked away on the first 'no.'" Although she is in a position now to join Equity, having been a member of SAG for more than six months, she says that she is going to wait until she gets an Equity part before she plunks down the initiation fee and starts paying dues. "I've been told that it's not worth it to join until you have to, and the people who tell me that are Equity members."

Mysterious as the process of getting that first union contract seems, actors do it every year. (There are currently 29,000 members of SAG, 19,000 members of Equity, and 31,000 members of AFTRA.) An unemployed actor working in the box office at a downtown theatre while *Man of La Mancha* was playing there, got cast as an Inquisitor when the production moved uptown. The stage manager had noticed him, knew he was an actor, and knew that he was six feet tall. "He asked me if I was interested in the part and I said, 'Hell, yes!' It was a walk-on with no lines, but I got my Equity card, I got paid, and I was in a Broadway show!" An actress working as an apprentice in a summer tent got her first Equity contract when one of the female dancers ran away with the lead in the show and the producer needed a couple of replacements fast. Others plan more carefully for union membership: "When I landed in New York I had planned to study for at least a year before I even attempted to look for work. I had some money saved up, which I called my union fund, and when I had enough in the fund I joined AFTRA. Now I can join the other unions when I want to."

Once you have joined a union, be sure to keep your dues paid up. Familiarize yourself with the rules, attend union meetings, and take advantage of whatever benefits the union offers: job information (both acting and nonacting), free courses and seminars, advice on work-related problems, and if you are a member of Equity, "a free pair of shoes once a year if you are unemployed in Equity's jurisdiction." You'll probably need them.

Union membership does not always guarantee that a job will be waiting for you. Once you join the union, you simply join a different line at tryouts. Now you will be number 191 in an open Equity call for a production that has already been cast, and after six hours of waiting your name will be called, and you will have a two-minute interview with someone (most likely not with a producer or director, but with a "representative"), hand in your picture and résumé for a filing system in the sky, and be out on the street again in a flash. The unions string a fence between one set of unemployed actors and another. "If I waited around to get cast in union films I would end up being an extra all my life.

You have to go out and lie and cheat on all the nonunion productions to get some experience. So I have a bunch of fake names that I use. Hope I don't get caught."

This is a suggestion from the director of a nonunion summer theatre:

Young performers and others are advised *not* to join Equity until they give it much thought; when they do, they restrict themselves from applying for many other jobs and throw themselves in with nineteen thousand other union members looking for jobs. With so many nonunion dinner theatres, summer theatres, regional theatres, road tours, et cetera, there is plenty of work for any actor with a lot of talent in non-Equity companies. Many of these pay well and some even better than Equity companies. A good non-Equity actor can work year-round in his chosen profession; however, it is very difficult for an Equity member to get even six months work with an Equity show or company because of the heavy competition among union members.

Where the Unions Are

Actors Equity Association (AEA)
1500 Broadway
New York, N.Y. 10036
212-869-8530

6430 Sunset Boulevard
Hollywood, Calif. 90028
213-462-2334

American Federation of Television and
  Radio Artists (AFTRA)
1350 Avenue of the Americas

advertising using your name or your picture or your voice. He can execute contracts for your services. He can collect money that belongs to you, and take his percentage from this money. He can hire and fire agents, and other managers. Although he is not required to do so in his contract, a manager may also advance you money against future earnings, handle your finances, buy your clothes, groom and coach you, buy your house in Hollywood, live with you, and love you. You, in turn, agree to devote yourself to your acting career.

In the contract both the length of the agreement and the commission that you will pay your manager, which has been known to range from 10 per cent to as much as 50 per cent, are left wide open for negotiation.

There is a case both for and against personal managers. The most obvious one is the case against. Young, innocent actors are forever being warned against getting involved with an unethical manager who comes on like Svengali, attaches himself to you like a parasite, and does absolutely nothing to help you—nothing that you can't do yourself. What this kind of manager does do, and does very well, is to take your money.

On the other side of the fence, there are many examples where a manager does have the best interests of the actor in mind. There is a legitimate bond between the two parties based on mutual friendship, trust, and belief, with a real exchange of services between actor and manager.

Cameo

ACTOR: I work with my manager. He is like an acting coach and a business manager and I pay him according to what I earn. It's a very good working relationship. He has incredible perceptions as to what's going on in the business, as well as with me and the development of my craft. He said in the beginning, "I can't do anything for you. If you don't do it yourself, it isn't going to get done." He is like a guidepost for me. Everybody has to have someone they can trust in this business and it's important that there is someone who works for you, who understands you, and with whom you can communicate. I can work with him on a song or a scene, or I can work with him on getting my apartment together. What you need is somebody who believes in you and somebody you believe in, and you can't buy that.

MANAGER: In my opinion, a contract with a manager is like a marriage license. You are stuck for as long as the two of you want to work together. And you don't enter into an agreement like this lightly. You have to know that the two of you believe in the product. I have to believe in the actor I'm managing, and he has to believe in me.

Traditionally, actors don't need managers until they are making a good deal of money, and then what they need is someone to handle their business affairs. I doubt that many young actors would really benefit from the services performed by a manager, and vice versa, except in an unusual case, such as the one described in the above cameo. A source of information for some managers' names and addresses can be obtained from the Conference of Personal Managers (Jack Segal, Secretary), 850 Seventh Avenue, New York, N.Y. 10021.

MAKING A LIVING
7

WHAT YOU WILL MAKE

You have been interviewed, you have cold read and auditioned, and you have been called back to audition again. You are told "Thanks very much, that was nice. We'll be in touch." You have waited, not exactly by the telephone, but you have waited to hear for weeks or even months. This time the call comes through, and you have landed the part. ("Landing" a part is like landing a fish—except that you are both fisherman and bait. Well, this time the fish are biting.) How much will you make?

The unions frequently renegotiate their contracts as they expire and so the salaries mentioned here are very likely to change—for the better. But the following will at least give you a general idea of what kind of money you can expect from the various avenues of employment. Also, these minimum-wage scales obviously do not take into account better terms and conditions of employment your agent could conceivably negotiate for and obtain from a producer.

Actors Equity Association has separate agreements with stock companies, dinner theatres, resident theatres, Off-Broadway and Broadway theatres. Each agreement sets forth minimum-wage scales and working conditions for the players employed.

Stock companies, League of Resident Theatres (LORT) members, and dinner theatres are rated by the AEA according to their potential weekly gross receipts. The higher this rating is, the higher an actor's minimum salary will be. For example, if you get a part in an "X" rated stock-company production, you will get $213 per week; "Y" companies pays $173 per week; "Z" companies $157 per week (or if you are "jobbed" in, you will get an extra $39 per week).

Dinner theatres are classified as large, medium, small, or petit, and scale wages start at $202.40 and go down to $135 a week.

If you are employed in a theatre on the LORT circuit that has an "A" rating, you will get $202.45 per week. If the theatre has a "D" rating, your wages will be a weekly $137.50.

Off-Broadway must currently pay actors $150 a week with a sliding scale that goes into effect when the weekly receipts of the theatre exceed $7000. Broadway pays a minimum of $265 a week. If you are in the chorus line or have a no-line walk-on, your pay will be quite a bit less.

AFTRA has negotiated a contract which guarantees a principal in a half-hour soap opera $203.50. A principal is an actor who has more than five lines to speak—the part is called an "over 5." (A line is defined in the contract as "not more than ten words, and a part of a line shall be considered a line.") "Under 5s" and extras are paid much less, naturally.

What is likely to happen if you land a running part in a soap opera is that your agent will negotiate a guaranteed number of performances for you in the thirteen-week cycle (soaps, series, commercials all run in thirteen-week cycles). For example, if there are twenty-six performances in the thirteen-week cycle, you will be guaranteed payment, at whatever salary your agent has managed to get for you, for twenty-six half-hour episodes, whether you work that many times or not. It is conceivable that you might be called upon to work only twenty-three times in those thirteen weeks; if so, the extra money is gravy. On the other hand, if you are called upon to work *more* than twenty-six times, you will be paid additional wages for it.

The television commercial is an area where actors can make a lot of money (if they are either lucky or famous) or at least keep the rent paid. At this writing, a filmed commercial for television pays $165.90 on camera, and $123.90 for a voice-over. This is a day's pay, or "session fee," and covers your payment for one commercial. If you spend a day making a commercial, and two or three commercials are ultimately made from the film shot during the session, you will be paid an additional $165.90 for each separate commercial made.

The payments (residuals) made to a player for the use and reuse of commercials is based upon how the commercial is used, i.e., whether the commercial is used as a program commercial or as a "wild spot," and upon the scope of the commercial, i.e., the number of cities it is shown in. A "Class A" program commercial will be shown in over twenty cities (New York, Chicago, and Los Angeles each count as eleven cities, so you can tell by this that population is really what is being considered). And Class A use of a commercial will pay you residuals each time the commercial is aired in a thirteen-week cycle, up to a total of $956. If the commercial is used in another thirteen-week cycle, the residual payments begin again at the beginning. Commercials given Class B or C use don't pay residuals. You will be given an initial fee to make the commercial, and this fee will cover unlimited use of the commercial in a thirteen-week cycle. The minimum fee for these wild-spot commercials is determined by a very intricate system which involves computing the cities and their unit weights and coming up with a rate in dollars. One agent feels that this kind of commercial can be harmful for an actor: "I don't think it's worthwhile for actors to do these commercials unless, of course, they are guaranteed a whole lot more money up front. Because the advertiser buys unlimited use of the commercial, it can be shown on television again and again until you want to throw up if you see a certain actor's face one more time! This kind of overexposure can really be bad." All commercials are retired after twenty-one months.

If you get a part in a television series, there are several contracts to cover this kind of employment under the Screen Actors Guild Television Agreement, depending upon the length of a show (half hour, one hour, one and a half hours, etc.), and the number of shows guaranteed the actor. For instance, you can be guaranteed thirteen half-hour episodes, in which case you will currently be paid a minimum salary of $604 for each episode. Or you might be guaranteed employment in *not less than seven* episodes, in which case you'll get $690 an episode.

In addition there is the whole realm of reruns. The networks, unfortunately, have become rerun addicts, to the great disadvantage of actors as well as of the television audience. Whereas reruns were originally used for the summer months, they are now being used midseason, during the spring, and at Christmastime. A proliferation of reruns obviously means fewer job opportunities for actors, and much less of a chance for beginning actors to get those first few crucial job breaks. If a show is rerun on television during prime time, an actor is paid 50 per cent of his original salary (plus a certain percentage of the difference between minimum wage and what he was originally paid). The third time the show is aired, the actor will get 40 per cent (plus percentage) of his original salary. The fourth, fifth, and sixth runs pay an actor 25 per cent, the seventh, eighth, and ninth runs pay him 15 per cent, and the tenth and all other reruns a final 15 per cent. Very few shows are rerun more than three times, but there are exceptions. If the show is not rerun during prime time, the percentage the actor receives for the second and third telecasts is slightly less than the above.

There are a variety of contracts for work in films—called "theatrical motion pictures" (as opposed to television films and industrial films). You can be employed as a "day player" in a single role on a picture for $172.50 a day. You can be employed as a "Free-Lance Player" on a weekly basis at $604.00 per week. There are contracts for "Multiple Picture Players" and for "Contract" or "Term Players." A Term Player is employed for motion pictures or television films for a guaranteed ten out of thirteen weeks under a contract which may not specify any role, picture, or series. In 1975, a Term Player currently got $517.50 per week—or if classified as a "beginner" (no professional experience as an actor, not including extra work or chorus work), $232.50 per week. There is a contract for Free-Lance Players whose salaries are less than $1500 per week, and the guarantee for the picture is less than $25,000. There is a contract for Free-Lance Players whose salary is more than $1500 per week, and the sky's the limit at that point. This kind of money talk will happen when *who* you are matters more than anything else; when you are "box office," as they say in Hollywood, and will be commanding salary plus percentages. Strangely enough, on the huge multistar pictures, the stars often will work for scale plus a percentage (called points) of the gross, which is figured after the entire investment in the picture has been recouped.

Finally, to get back to earth, if you are hired to perform in an industrial film (motion pictures such as documentaries, sales motion pictures, educational and training pictures, etc., made for nonprofit organizations you will earn a minimum wage of $150 a day on camera and $138 each day off camera; if you are hired by the week, you will get $525 on camera each week, and $483 off camera. There are provisions in the contract for compensation if the film is later shown on television.

All union contracts specify very clearly when and how an actor is to be paid by the producer. If a particular producer fails to pay his actors on time, he will be penalized. If an actor is not paid on time, he must bring it to the appropriate union's attention for recourse.

INCOME TAX

If you have any aspirations of being a successful actor, you should begin planning right away to deal with your partner, Uncle Sam. Once you start making real money, you will find that the IRS is right there with its hand out, waiting for at least 20 per cent and as much as 50 per cent of your gross earnings. When you are making a living at your profession, a great deal of your *real income* is not what you gross, but what you don't have to pay the government. There is a large difference between tax avoidance and tax evasion and tax avoidance is absolutely legal.

The tax system is pretty rough on actors who usually make their money in big chunks, and then go for long periods when little or no money is coming in. Take, for example, an actor who has a running part in a soap opera and is getting paid $250 for each half-hour show he appears on. One week he may work only once, so his salary for that week will be $250; the tax withheld for that week will be calculated as if he made $250 for fifty-two weeks a year. The next week he might work on five shows in a row and make a total of $1250. He will then be taxed as if he made $1250 for fifty-two weeks a year. What many actors will do in this and similar cases is ask to be paid a certain amount of money each week, for example $500, to help balance out his tax payments and keep an even cash flow. This is just one example of why it is important for you to have a good accountant who is knowledgeable about the ins and outs of the tax system.

The experts in this field are tax accountants. Get one. For the modest fee that a good accountant will charge, your savings on tax payments will be worth it. A decent accountant will cost you $100 or less, and will be someone who will stay with you, help you plan a program, and advise you as to how accurately to claim your deductions. Unlike a lot of businesses, an actor is in business for himself. Practically everything that you do, and the expenses that you incur, will relate to your business and hence be legitimate deductions. If you earn $12,000 one year, and half of it constitutes legitimate business expenses, your tax bracket will be lowered considerably and the money you are allowed to keep will be more substantial.

If you want to go the self-help route, the best book to buy and use as a reference book is J. K. Lasser's *Your Income Tax* which is updated annually. However, once the money starts to come in, it is advisable to work with an accountant.

Back Stage prints a weekly column devoted to actors and income taxes, and it is definitely worth reading. Harry

Linton, a tax consultant who writes the column, will also answer questions by mail (c/o *Back Stage*, 165 West 46th Street, New York, N.Y. 10036; enclose a stamped self-addressed envelope). Unions will occasionally sponsor seminars on some aspect of the subject of taxes; AFTRA, for example, gave a course on recordkeeping for its members not long ago.

SURVIVING IN THE MEANTIME

Tom Millott, a director/manager, proposed the following test for young actors who are considering acting as a profession:

> The first thing you should do if you want to go into this business is to spend an hour in front of the mirror finding out what you really look like. Once you get over the shock, and once you have taken all the negative things away, decide if you think you would pay ten dollars to see You. If you would, then you are on the right track. If you wouldn't, then you had better find out if there is anything else in your life you would like to do and go for that. But if there isn't anything else, and you still want to act, know that you have three strikes against you before you begin, because the theatre and the entertainment world is built on sex appeal. If you are not physically attractive, then you have to look again and ask yourself: What do I have that makes me so special the public would be willing to pay ten dollars to see me? Can I dance like Fred Astaire? Can I sing like Judy Garland?

> Then, if you finally make the decision to go into the business, and you really believe that that's where you want to be, where you have to be, then there's no

problem. But you have to know. You just have to know that you've got it, that you've got what they want.

If this is the first thing you should do as an actor, the second and equally important test of your survival potential is to ask yourself a two-part question: What can I do to earn a living while I am trying to make it as an actor, and what am I going to do to earn a living if I don't make it as an actor?

You are going to have to answer that question, because, unless you happen to be one of the lucky ones, you are likely never to make it. The "meantime" is going to be a large part of the time, and the question of survival will never cease to dog your heels. It can be very romantic, idealistic, and exciting to starve and struggle when you are eighteen or twenty-five, but it probably won't be quite so much fun when you are forty-five or fifty and unemployed. You will have to get yourself a useful, practical second career, a skill that is marketable in general, one that you can fall back on and one that you can count on to pull you through hard times.

I asked one woman what made her give up her acting career, and she explained, "I had just finished doing a play in New York and was driving home that night with two other actors from the cast. It was very late. We were all pretty exhausted, and no one was talking. Suddenly, out of nowhere, one of them said, 'You never know when you're going to work again.' And it just hit me. I realized that I just didn't have the physical or emotional stamina to endure waking up the next morning, combing my hair, putting on my face, and starting all over again."

You will often be faced with periods of unemployment when you will be forced to fend for yourself in the part-time or even full-time job world. The ideal solution is to get yourself a job that will leave you free enough to be able to pursue your acting career, take classes, make the rounds, go to auditions, and perform whenever and wherever you get the chance.

This perfect job, however, is not easy to come by, and there will inevitably be conflicts. Most employers are not apt to be sympathetic to an employee who wants to take off for a couple of hours in the afternoon to go to an audition. One actress, who decided that she wanted to work full time for a while in order to save up enough money so that she could concentrate on her acting career, found out that she was better off *not* telling potential employers that she was an actress: "Whenever I mentioned my acting, the guy's face would go blank and he'd tell me that the company wouldn't want to hire someone who might up and quit any day. So I got smart and stopped mentioning it and got a job."

Part-time jobs are usually the best solution to making money to pay the rent and keep your shoes well heeled. Waiting on tables, bartending, taxi driving, modeling, hat checking, telephone soliciting, typing, being a stenographer, a substitute teacher or a carpenter are some of the myriad ways actors and actresses make ends meet. Read the trades for "help wanted" ads, and explore the temporary agencies which specialize in filling temporary office positions.

It might be worth your while to investigate the television quiz show as a means of solving, at least temporarily, your financial binds. The trick is to figure out which show your intelligence is geared for, and which game you can play the best, and then apply to that show as a contestant. Apparently, the people who do the hiring on these shows like to hire actors because they make good contestants—they can be lively, enthusiastic, bubbly, and attractive on cue. The catch is that you are *not* supposed to tell the talent coordinator that you are an actor—but if you are bartending at night, you are a bartender, right? Then you will have to go through a long screening process that might include a written test, then an interview, after which you will have to play the game several times on camera before you are chosen to be a contestant. From watching the shows, you will be able to figure out the character you will be expected to play—a cross between Miss or Mr. Personality and a jack-in-the-box—as well as the rules of the game. And if you win, your financial worries might be over for six months. If you lose, you will at least be the recipient of a consolation prize—for instance, a case of instant onion soup to warm your belly on a cold winter's night. Good luck.

WORKING AS AN EXTRA

The Screen Actors Guild has jurisdiction over extra players employed in the production of motion pictures or filmed commercials based in New York, and has established that actors who are registered as extra players with certain designated casting agencies shall have preference when a producer is filling a call for extras. (Agents don't handle extra work because they are not allowed to take commission from an extra actor's wages.) In Los Angeles, there is a separate union for extra players, the Screen Extras Guild (SEG), and there are hundreds of actors who are members and eke out a living as professional extras.

The ruling that extras must belong to SAG or SEG (or join within thirty days of first employment as an extra) is very strict because, otherwise, producers would hire family and friends, depriving those who are paying union dues.

An actor can be hired as a "General Extra" (the

performance of ordinary business) and will receive $47.50 per day; a "Special Ability Extra" (dancing, swimming, skating, riding a horse, playing sports, handling camels and elephants, etc.) will get an additional $10 per day; and an extra who has a "silent bit" (performing pantomime essential to the staging of a scene) will get $95 for a day's work.

If you work as an extra in a commercial, you will either be paid a lump sum for unlimited use of the commercial, or a session fee for a thirteen-week cycle, and then another fee if the commercial is used beyond thirteen weeks.

UNEMPLOYMENT INSURANCE AND WELFARE

It can probably be safely stated that every actor working today has stood in line in an unemployment office in New York or Hollywood at one point or another, waiting to sign for a check. He or she might have arrived at the office in a chauffeur-driven Mercedes or had to borrow money to hop the subway to get there; both are there for the same reason.

In order to qualify for unemployment insurance, you will have to have worked at a job or jobs which are covered by unemployment insurance. You will have to have worked at least a certain number of weeks (in New York it is twenty weeks in a fifty-two-week period) and earned a certain amount of money, and then been "laid off" because of "lack of work." For instance, if you have a twenty-four-week run in a series, and it terminates, you are eligible for unemployment insurance. You will then be able to collect this insurance, which is paid biweekly, and is the equivalent of half the amount of money you earned each week you worked, with the current ceiling at $95, for twenty-six weeks. If, during this period, you are lucky enough to pick up a week's work, you simply do not collect your insurance for that week. In times of high unemployment, an additional thirteen weeks will be granted to those collecting.

After your unemployment insurance runs out, and if you cannot get any work at all, your only alternative is to apply for welfare. You will be required to prove to the caseworker at the welfare office that you have no visible means of support, that you, in fact, are destitute; or get a doctor to certify that you are mentally ill or physically unable to work. This is a desperate and depressing last resort, and one which I hope you will not have to consider.

Instead of ending this book on such a low note, or writing a well-meaning but unrealistic conclusion filled with upbeat, encouraging phrases, I feel that the best kind of conclusion could be "written" by some actors and actresses who have been through the mill described in the book and have drawn their own conclusions about the acting profession. They are all different, but they have something in common that will be helpful to anyone starting out in their careers—a belief in their own talent, a determination to succeed, and a realistic view of themselves and the world they inhabit.

Cameo
Warren Oates—Actor

If you start out being envious or jealous because somebody else is working and you're not, it will get to be a bad hang-up for you and you will begin to worry more about that than what you should be doing for yourself. You make rounds. You go around and see people. Of course they aren't going to want you. Nobody wants a new face, particularly agents. Starting somebody out is extra work, difficult work, fruitless work. So what you learn right away is that nobody is going to help you. Between you and your friends, you may help each other survive, but nobody helps you because everybody is trying to help themselves. It's a real self-help occupation.

When I came out of the Marine Corps and started college, I got into student plays, not out of any desire of my own but because an English teacher said you ought to do this part in the play. I did it and began to like it very much. I got hooked on the fact that it gave me significance around campus. I wasn't a quarterback, I was an actor.

My first job was as an extra on a television show in New York. I ran into a buddy of mine at this place called the Hayes Registry, where every actor paid two bucks a month and had an answering service, and he told me that they were casting for the *Jackie Gleason Show*, and I said "beautiful" or something to that effect, and he said "but you better run." And so I ran from Forty-Sixth Street to Fifty-Seventh Street and I was one of the first ten guys in the door so I got the job. I did a lot of extras.

I studied with Herbert Berghof for a year and got malnutrition because I didn't take a part-time job. I finally figured I'd better so I could eat. I worked at the "21" Club checking hats and coats. It was an ideal job because it kept my days free and my mind jumping. Life didn't stop because I wanted to be an actor. It was fun.

Daniel Petrie was directing the *U.S. Steel Hour* and there was a part in it that was right up my alley. I figured that the only way to get into that office was to pull a stunt so I ran up the stairs to the fifth floor and I ran into his office and told the secretary that I had a hundred-and-fifty-five-pound package for Mr. Petrie. She said, "What is it?" I told her I didn't know. And so she called Dan to the door. "What is this," he said, "you have a hundred-and-fifty-five-pound package for me?" I said, "Yes, it's me!" It broke him up. I didn't get the part.

My agent stole a script off a guy's desk one time because I couldn't get it, and I ended up working for Sam Peckinpah. And the more I worked for Sam Peckinpah, the more I worked for Sam Peckinpah. And that's about the way it's been for me.

There aren't any rules to this business. If I wanted to sell insurance, I'd go about it the same way. It's one of the few occupations in the world where you don't need a license. All you have to do is say, "Here I am. I'm an actor, and I want a job." And along the way you'll find out it isn't about being successful. It's about doing something that you have a compulsion to do. And I think all the laws of society apply. You have to be legal, straightforward, and polite. The same way your grandmother raised you.

I know one thing: there are more bad men in movies than leading men. So I didn't go for the leading men, I went for the bad men. I played bad men for a long time, still am. It's all acting to me. It's a chance to make a full person out of a one-dimensional character. That's the only joy there is. And you know the beginning and the middle and the end of the story and you know you're really not going to be shot. It's the easiest job in the world, except for the hours.

Cameos
Jacquelyn Hyde—Actress

I started out in New York when I was fourteen. I
looked nineteen so I answered an ad for a summer stock
company, and they signed me on as a resident ingenue. I
went into stock for ten weeks and did ten shows back to
back. At that point I had never studied. I was very good
right away. I had some quality on the stage; I was
different. Then I started studying with a woman in New
York. She saw me in a play Off-Off-Off-Broadway and
came backstage afterward and told me that she would
like to work with me. I went to her apartment five or six
days a week after school. I remember her sitting me down
and saying, "It's what's behind the lines, the words are
just words, you have to find out what the subtext is." I
worked with her for three years—almost to the point of a
nervous breakdown. But I knew she was giving me
something.

Finally, after three years, I decided it was time to break
away, and it was time for me to go out and see if I could
get work. I didn't dare tell her in person, so I wrote her a
long letter and she wrote me a long letter back telling me
that I was selling out to the commercial world. Which
was a crock. You can't be creative sitting in your
bedroom. You have to get out and do it. And you want to
earn a living at it. At first you think they are paying you
for nothing, because you are doing what you want to do
anyway, but after a while you know you should be paid
for it because you are knocking your brains out.

I did a lot of stock. I worked most of the playhouses on
the east coast. I did Tallulah Bankhead's tour. That was
an incredible experience. She was old and tired and sick

but her timing was still impeccable. And for thirteen weeks I worked with her. But nothing ever happened to me in terms of film. I mean, a small group of people thought I was great but I never seemed to connect with anything. I came close to things. At that time Barbara Harris was doing *Oh Dad, Poor Dad* at the Phoenix, and they were looking for a replacement for her and they liked me. I went back to read for it three times and then the author decided that he wanted an actress that had a completely different look. It's a flip of the cards. If I had gotten it, I probably would have made it big then—this was eleven years ago. The girl who got the part was Patricia Hardy. Later, Ernie Pintoff wrote a script that was partially about me and, of course, everybody assumed that I would play the part. But Ernie decided that I wasn't right to play myself and another girl got the part. And the weird thing about these two incidents is that she and I couldn't be less alike. We are like negatives of each other.

As I look back on it now, I think there were two things that prevented me from making it early. Part of it is that flip of the cards; part of it was the fact that I can't play small roles. I'm too forceful, too specific. So when I would read for a Broadway show, it would be for the lead. I was not a star, but I wasn't an ingenue either because I didn't look like one, so it was difficult to place me. And if there was a role that fit me, they'd veto me because the star wouldn't want me around. So I couldn't work at all.

The rejection is what you have to deal with. It is the most humiliating experience I know. Part of you is totally destroyed. The other part of you still believes that you are wonderful and special. It is a tremendous ego that can say, I am a very special person and I have this talent to give. You have to hang on to your dreams. What happened to me was that I would go through periods of extreme depression. There were times when I couldn't face going out to see people. I stayed home and fantasized what it would be like *if* I got this part or that part.

I supported myself by doing odd jobs. I worked as a demonstrator in Macy's, in the toy department; I sold makeup; I demonstrated a soda siphon in Bloomingdale's. And sometimes I just didn't give a damn and borrowed money from my friends. I knew a lot of people in the business. I was always "going somewhere" and people would say, "Oh, look at Jackie! She's just marvelous." It was kind of an aura and it didn't have anything to do with reality. It was an unreal life.

I knew a couple of casting people who introduced me to other people, and the tide seemed to turn. Two weeks after I arrived, I went up to Orange County to do *Long Day's Journey* and *A Thousand Clowns*. And I got fantastic reviews. There was something in the emotional climate out here that made it easier for me to function. I got an agent almost immediately after that—I went for an interview and got signed and he didn't do a damned thing for me. He was all big talk and a lot of promises. And I didn't demand things of him the way I would now. I think I was a little "chicken." I also thought it was so wonderful that I had an agent after being out here for such a short time. I finally got angry because he simply wasn't doing his job and so, after about eight months, we had a kind of mutual firing.

My first feature was a Woody Allen picture called *Take the Money and Run*. Everyone had said that there was no way I could get a feature film unless I had some film on me that people could see. But the timing was right. The same casting director I had met when I first came out here was casting the picture for Woody Allen. He called my agent and set up an appointment and I got the part. I read for the producers. I didn't need that piece of film on me. And I got great reviews but nothing happened. Then I got a part in *They Shoot Horses, Don't They?* because the producer had seen all the dailies of *Take the Money* and liked my work. I didn't even have to read for the director. I was co-starred and it gave me some reputation. But I was still starving!

Part of my problem when I came out here was the fact that I was versatile. There were a lot of different parts I could play and I became confusing to the gentlemen on the other side of the desk.

Getting the casting people to come and see you takes an agent who is willing to spend time on the phone forcing people to come. Or else you have to start a campaign on your own and do the corniest thing in the world—get some picture postcards and print the information about the play on the back. And if I were well reviewed, I would spend my last twenty-five dollars Xeroxing the reviews and sending out the biggest mailing in the world, and I would send it three or four or five times. There's no other way that they are going to get to know you. Hollywood is not a theatre town, but last year we did *Father's Day* and got every casting director and a long list of directors and producers to see it. My agents took the time to do it. And I consider that play a turning point for me—nine years later, and all sorts of roles later. As a direct result of *Father's Day* I got *Love, American Style* and *Queen of the Stardust Ballroom* with Maureen Stapleton.

One thing that actors have to contend with on a set, besides the work that you are going to do in front of the camera, is the whole social setup. You go to work early in the morning, your eyes are half shut, someone is going to be fooling around with your face and your hair, and these people are going to be talking to you. They are real people. And you have to deal with them on some kind of social level, and at the same time you have to keep your concentration. That's one of the toughest parts of making films. The situation is like a big party. You are stuck on a sound stage with fifty other people, and it's very personal. It takes a long time to be able to walk onto a set and adjust. Each time you feel like you're walking into a party and you don't know anyone, and there's that terrible moment of fear. I think it hangs a lot of actors up. You have to learn how to be social but not too social.

Ten years ago as an actress who wanted to be totally creative and play a lot of different parts, I wouldn't have wanted to do a television series. Who wants to do the same thing every week? But I don't say that any more. A series would establish a name for me and give me security, and there would be millions of people all over the country who would know who I am. Then I could break out of the mold and do different things. Lee Grant came out here to do *Peyton Place*, and she's done every conceivable kind of role since then. You don't have to get stuck in a series in a way that eliminates you for any other work. What you have to say is: "I've got a series and I am going to be the best goddamn actress in the series I can be." You can be just as creative within the confines of a not-so-creative situation and come out of it with the money and some reputation.

I have been thinking about what an actor goes through when he starts out in this business, and I almost want to say to young actors, "Go Away!" And yet, when you find things beginning to happen for you, you realize that you got through it all, and so you can't turn around and say to a kid, don't do it. But you have to learn to be a survivor. And the doubts and insecurity never really leave you. I had an interview today. They were obviously interested, but said they were looking for a different type. I might get the part, but I left thinking maybe I wasn't so good, maybe I would have been better at two in the afternoon than at ten in the morning.

Warren Finnerty—Actor

If I were a nice guy I probably could get a lot of little bits on the stage.

I know in terms of myself that my problem as an actor has been a social thing. I know through my own experience in casting a play that directors use their friends. I guess most directors do that. But I'm shy and I don't want to be friendly with anyone. I thought that I'd just have to be better than anybody else and that would be enough, but it wasn't true. I'm withdrawn, particularly when I'm in new situations. I've seen actors go up and really talk to critics and be friendly with them, but if I see a critic I just walk the other way.

I know that it's my fault, both in and out of the theatre. But acting is something I do well, and why my personality has to get in the way is a drag. You have to go out and hustle and I just lie in my pad waiting for the phone to ring. I'm as good an actor as I am because I am the kind of person I am, but maybe that's a cop-out, maybe I could be successful and good at the same time.

The main thing is that I think it is such a waste that I'm not working and doing the things I should be doing. I want to act. I'm an entertainer. I'm a clown and a fool, and I can stand up in a room full of people and amuse them. It's my life's work, and if you are not doing your life's work, then you are really not living.

Cindy Williams—Actress

When I was in high school I was studying to be a nurse, despite the fact that I have no mind for academic training. The only classes I cared about were art history, drama, and English. I worked really hard but I thought, This is no fun if I have to go through eight years of college in order to become something. We happened to have a sensational drama coach at the high school. I got into his class by a fluke because I auditioned for a PTA talent show, and he spotted me and wanted to put me into his advanced class. I said, "Well, maybe I'll take it next year." And I did. Meanwhile I'm thinking, I'm going to be a nurse. I'm a humanitarian and I can help people and I liked the idea of the costume and the tag and the drama of it, working in the emergency ward, calming people down. I finally realized I couldn't do it when we started to cut open frogs. I felt sorry for the frog and I'd faint. So I said, no more; that's it for nursing. By this time we were doing plays like *The Madwoman of Chaillot*, which I had a big part in, and *Diary of Anne Frank* and I was Anne Frank. And when I'd get a laugh or a response from the audience, it was just like old home week for me. Acting came easy for me.

Then I went to LACC, which is a junior college with a terrific theatre arts department, and within the context of that situation I think that's when I decided I could do it. I did eight big plays, I did character parts, and the competition was incredible—we started with seventy-seven people in a class and ended up with thirteen.

You have another transitional point when you leave college, and it's awful. I think colleges should have seminars to teach the students what to do if they really feel they have the talent and the physical and mental stamina to carry themselves through the gambit of Hollywood. The film business in Hollywood is a clique, and there's an in-circle, and you have to get into that in-circle. It can be done and it can be done with great finesse, without losing too much of yourself, especially if you know that you are talented. If you feel that in your heart of hearts, it will win out, no matter what, the talent will win out.

When I got out of college I knew nothing about the business of getting work as an actress. And I am not good at going into an office and saying, "Look!" I worked as a waitress and did odd jobs and the dreams started fading in and out and I thought, Oh, it will never work. If it's going to work, it's going to be by chance. I thought about getting the book from the Screen Actors Guild and going down the list of agents and calling them, but I knew that was never going to work. What happened to me was I went for an interview for a student film-making job. It was a government-sponsored program and the man who was running it could only hire people with poverty-stricken ethnic backgrounds who knew something about film. If you got hired you got three hundred dollars a month and you learned something about editing and other film techniques. I thought this was great; I had the talent, I was very poor, I'd go in and get the job. Well, after my interview the man told me he couldn't hire me because I wasn't ethnic enough or poor enough. He said,

"What do you really want to do this for?" I said, "Because I want to act and I figure that if I can make my own films I can put myself in front of the camera." He said, "Then you want to be an actress and that's what you should do." I said, "How?" and was about to leave when he wrote down two names and told me to call these people; they were young producers. I thought for sure that this would be a quickie on the couch, but he gave me the card and I stuck it in my pocket anyway. About a month later, I found it and I called them. They were both out of town but the secretary asked me for my name and number. And a month after that, we were all sitting at dinner at my mother's and my dad answered the phone and said that a producer wanted to talk to me. And the producer said, "I want to see you tomorrow." I said yes. I didn't even own a skirt—I just had blue jeans and T shirts—so my sister and I went to some department store and I got this really raunchy skirt and I went to see him and he liked me. He took me upstairs and introduced me to his partner, who talked to me and then told me to turn around; he told me I was cute, like a pudgy Barbara Harris. And they started sending me to agents.

My experience with these agents was incredibly awful. I had one interview on a fire escape facing the sun. I can't see in a dark room, let alone with the sun in my eyes, so I asked if I could put my sunglasses on, and he said he couldn't see my face with the glasses on it. Then he said he couldn't use me because he had too many girls like me. Other agents would want to drive to the beach and smoke dope. I finally got to the point where I didn't want to meet any more agents. They finally sent me to a good agent who is intelligent, wonderful, respected, and he asked me to show him a couple of scenes. I had no film on me and it's practically unheard of that an agent will take you if you don't have film on you. So I worked for about a month with a couple of other actors and we came into the office and did these scenes. And they took me!

My first job was a *Room 222*. I guess now an actor's first job might be a gig on *Kojak* or *The Mary Tyler Moore Show*. In those days it was *Room 222*. They'd always give you a break on *Room 222*. Then I did a Roger Corman film called *Gaff*, which is one of the favorite things I've ever done. Ben Vereen and Tally Shire and Bud Cort are in it. It was shot on location in New Mexico and I had a terrific funny part and I was thoroughly spoiled. And things were happening. I worked enough to support myself. I did commercials, and episodic television and comedy shows, and I was in *Drive, He Said* for a couple of seconds. And I never got frightened once, I was never at a point in my career when I couldn't face going back and waiting on tables. I'm not afraid of *not* making it. That's an important factor; to be totally unafraid of failure. They sense it in this town; they can smell it a mile away.

I got a series, then I got *Travels with My Aunt*, then *American Graffiti*, and then *The Conversation*.

And now I'm in the "big wait." It is like another transition for me because I can't go back and do certain things. I have to wait. I've been asked to do a couple of television series and I've turned them down. If I do one of them, I'll be stuck for three years. I would rather do movies, and then when I'm around forty do a bang-up television series. I know if I do it now, that's the end. I just sense it.

Recently, there have been five big movie projects that I've been up for and gotten right up to the line, and they've just not seen it because I'm an unusual type and they say, "We'll take the other actress but we want you to know we think you're very good." It's hell. I got to the point where if I walked into an office I was so sensitive to what was happening, I knew, I could go out of my body and flash ahead to what they were going to do and say. I won't go on interviews any more unless it's with the director I want to see, because I have nothing to lose. It has gotten to the point where it has got to be special. I'm going to have to have a special film. I have yet to show my own brightness and nothing else is going to matter to me. I just have to wait.

I belong to two theatres, Theatre West and the Actors' Studio. That's very important for an actor. You have got to find a place, a workshop, or theatre group where you can go and work. You have to integrate with other actors and get that feedback.

I talked to my publicist today and I said that I wanted a low profile this month; I feel that I have no anonymity, no privacy. I didn't want to go on any more talk shows. I just want to do my acting. I sleep in my bed at night and I think, People know where I'm sleeping! "Cindy," he said, "that's what you give up." And he's right! I was on a talk show last night and I will never do another one again. I asked the host not to ask me certain questions and those were what he asked me about. He boxed me into a corner, and I knew I was screwed up when I left the show. I didn't know where my identity belonged, and this is where a lot of actors get messed up. I was thinking, I am not really famous, and yet people recognize me. It's all happening, it could be happening, but maybe it will never happen. Maybe I'll have to take a series.

I leave the talk show and go outside, and a little boy asks me for my autograph and I feel it's my last touch with innocence because kids think it's so wonderful. He says, "It's to Mike." I write, "To Mike," and I look at him and I think, Should I say any more? Should I say, Always? I decide not to, and I sign it and walk away, and he says, "Miss Williams, you didn't sign your name. This isn't your name." I look at it and I had signed it Cindy Always.

A selection of books published by Penguin is listed on the following page.

For a complete list of books available from Penguin in the United States, write to Dept. DG, Penguin Books, 299 Murray Hill Parkway, East Rutherford, New Jersey 07073.

For a complete list of books available from Penguin in Canada, write to Penguin Books Canada Limited, 2801 John Street, Markham, Ontario L3R 1B4.

THE STANISLAVSKI SYSTEM:
THE PROFESSIONAL TRAINING OF AN ACTOR

Sonia Moore
Preface by Sir John Gielgud and
Foreword by Joshua Logan

This handbook, the first simplified guide to Stanislavski's teachings, has long been a favorite among students and teachers of acting. Now, to bring it up to date in the light of recent books and articles published in the Soviet Union, Sonia Moore has made revisions that include a new section on emotional memory. She stresses the method of physical actions as the key to emotional memory and to organic behavior on the stage. She also places more emphasis on the actor's use of his body in the immediate expression of inner processes and urges her readers to study the system as a whole, without isolating its elements.

SOME OTHER THEATER BOOKS FROM PENGUIN

Also available in Penguin editions are many of the greatest works of the theater from the past as well as the present. Here is a sampling from the list of Penguin dramatic works:

New York, N.Y. 10019
212-265-7700

1717 North Highland Avenue (eleventh floor)
Hollywood, Calif. 90028
213-461-8111

Screen Actors Guild (SAG)
551 Fifth Avenue
New York, N.Y. 10017
212-687-4623

7750 Sunset Boulevard
Hollywood, Calif. 90046
213-876-3030

AGENTS AND MANAGERS

6

I had an agent interested in me in Hollywood who told me that the whole thing out there for an actress was tits and ass—tits and ass! And if you don't have that, you have to make it on something else. So this agent tried to convince me to tell people that I was a member of some minority group, like the American Indians or the Puerto Ricans.

—AN ACTRESS

The image of the agent as the sleazy guy in the shiny suit whose office is in a telephone booth is long gone, although agents are still "flesh peddlers" and will probably always have a slightly tainted social image as a result. Agents today are more powerful than ever before, and the large agencies, which seem to be forever merging into larger conglomerates, have supplanted the film studios as power plants in the industry establishment. (In January 1975 Marvin Josephson Associates, parent to International Famous Agency, merged with Creative Management Associates to form International Creative Management, second in size only to the William Morris Agency.)

It can be said that the agencies control the business in

Hollywood because they control, or "handle" the talent—actors, directors, writers, and producers, as well as literary properties. It can also be said that these agencies create jobs for their clients by packaging projects—putting together a star, a writer, a director, and whoever else they can include in the deal for a film to sell the studios. The big agents are not just 10-per-cent men any more.

Most people would say that an unknown actor cannot get along in Hollywood without an agent, and that he will find himself floundering around on the beach, quite literally, if he doesn't have an agent representing him. It is true that Hollywood is not accessible to an actor without an agent the way New York is; there an actor can, and many do, get along very well without an agent. Manager Tom Millott says, "Look at it logically. Who needs an agent? Does an agent hire you? Has an agent ever hired anyone?" An actor can make the rounds in New York as his own agent; he can get information and appointments quite on his own. The business is concentrated and the acting community is more communal with an effective grapevine system of communication. "There isn't an audition I can't find. That's one of the things I learned in New York: no matter how much of a rat hole the theatre is or where it's hidden, actors always smell it out," said Harry Cohn.

In Hollywood the doors are closed—the doors to producers, directors, and casting directors—and the studios are surrounded by ten-foot fences with barbed wire running around the top and a guard at every gate. An actor's dream of running into a studio lot, grabbing a producer by the collar, and screaming, "Do something with me!" is nothing but a dream. You can't make the rounds in Hollywood alone because you don't have access to the vital information—who's casting what, where, when, and how—and that's because the agents have it. Even if you did manage to find out about an audition, you wouldn't be able to get in the door without an agent's introduction. Except for some general interviews held by casting directors for television commercials, you need an agent to "get the meeting."

"Getting an agent is obviously an important part of getting started in the business in Hollywood," says Mike Medavoy, formerly an agent for the International Famous Agency (IFA), who also admits that once he had established his "stable" of actors and had made a name for himself as a top agent, he no longer had the need, the time, or the inclination to scout for new talent. At the same time, Medavoy thinks that a large agency is a better choice for a young actor because it has more power than a smaller agency—and power means information. The large agencies get it first and know what's happening before it happens. Unfortunately, most young actors don't have this kind of choice to make. They cannot choose to have a big-time agent represent them. "Come back to me when you're a star!" is the line, as the legend goes, that Sue Mengers deals out to young unknowns. She is one of the most powerful agents in the business, earning as much as $200,000 a year with such clients as Barbra Streisand, Faye Dunaway, and Gene Hackman. Another ex-agent expands on this theme: "When I was an agent, I wouldn't take on anybody who wasn't well known. The company didn't want to represent an actor who wasn't known, and the actors I did represent didn't give me the time to push someone who was brand-new. It's a full-time job to get someone new started. When I was an agent, my level was trying to get leads in films for my actors. Some brand-new kid is not going to get the lead in a big studio picture."

For a young unknown actor, a large agency is not likely

to be of interest, first because they don't need you, and second because you can get lost in the shuffle where their first concern is getting work for the actors who command million-dollar salaries. The ideal choice would be a small agency that is looking for new talent, one that is interested in developing the careers of new actors and finding a market for them. Look for an agency that is not already handling a handful of actors of your own type. If you are a "young leading man" you obviously don't want an agent who handles other young leading men with whom you will have to compete in the job hustle.

The unions provide lists of their franchised agents, and most agents are franchised by SAG, AFTRA, and AEA. It's a long list and cutting it down to a feasible size presents some problems. How do you decide which agents to call on? One actor spent several hours at the New York Equity office looking at *The Player's Guide* (in Hollywood, it's *The Academy Directory*), a giant directory of actors' names listed according to type (Ingenues, Leading Men, Leading Women, Character Actors, etc.) and the entries include photographs and the names of their agents. "I tried to figure out which agents didn't already have a bunch of actors of my type, and made up a shopping list." Another actress simply asked every person she met for recommendations while making rounds and in classes at her acting school until she had a list of twenty agents to "attack."

The next step, once you have your list of agents, is to drop by the agent's office with a letter requesting an interview and enclosing your picture and résumé. This letter and the subsequent call you will make will be greatly enhanced if you can say that so-and-so recommended that you call. I cannot emphasize strongly enough how important personal connections are in this business: the more you have, the better off you will be. And that's why you "drop by" instead of simply mailing material to an agent's office and insist on an appointment so that you will be able to make some kind of contact. Keep at it and be as aggressive as you can manage. Even if nothing happens the first couple of tries, keep trying.

If an agent is interested in you, he is eventually going to want to see your work. He might ask you to audition for him in his office, in which case you will be asked to bring in (or do on the spot) a couple of monologues or scenes to show him what you can do. Or he might ask you to let him know when you are performing in something that he could see. The agent might be quite sincere about this, or it might be a polite way of dismissing you, but do what he asks in any case.

These "somethings" are showcases—productions of plays that are performed Off-Off-Broadway and its Hollywood equivalent with a limited run under a special Equity contract. Pay is minimal or nothing at all, but actors will work hard to land a decent part in a showcase, expressly for the purpose of asking agents to come and see them perform. One actor recounts his own experience: "When I got to the city, the first thing I did was a showcase. I had the lead in *The Rimers of Eldritch* which was a perfect part for me. The play has a large cast and we all went around to as many agents as we could with fliers, inviting them to the play. We were bound to think that some of them would come. Well, they didn't, not a one. They all said that they would try to make it but they never showed up. One agent did show up, although he wasn't one we had invited. But he saw me and recommended me to an agent he knew who didn't have anyone like me. And I met him and signed with him. It was a lucky break for me and a perfect move."

It is easy to see why agents don't attend these showcase productions with more enthusiasm. The unfortunate fact is that a large majority of them add up to a dull evening: the play is new; the theatre is old, uncomfortable, hard to get to; and the production is amateurish. Unless an agent is really anxious to see your work, it's going to take a lot of persistence, persuasion, and just plain stubborn endurance on your part to keep at it, to keep working until you hit the right combination of part, play, and interested agent.

Other kinds of work can also serve as showcases for actors. A good commercial can serve you well, often without your being aware of it, and so can a principal part in a soap opera. Be sure to notify agents when you are going to be on, and ask them to watch.

If a Hollywood agent is interested in handling you, you will be asked to sign an exclusive-management contract with him, but in New York, the system works differently. There, the agents often do not sign actors right away, but simply submit them for various jobs. Once an actor starts to make it commercially, an agent will then want to sign him up. An actor says, "I'm not signed by anybody, but there are several agents who send me out for jobs when they have them. I don't think you need an agent until you get too busy. When three agents call you up for the exact same job and you have to tell two of them that so-and-so called you first, it is time for you to sign with an agent—the one who's working hardest for you, of course." The basic reason for this is lack of work. Agents don't readily sign new clients because they are hard pressed to get work for the actors they have signed already.

If an agent thinks you're a "good commercial type" and starts submitting you for jobs, it is important that you follow through. One actor assured me:

Agents get very upset if you miss a call they send you on. The casting director will have your name on a list and who sent it, and it won't look good if you don't show up. The agent won't like it, and it's very likely that you will drop down on his list. I don't know if it's a written list or a mental list, but to keep on it you show up for calls and you go back and see the agent regularly. I will always ask an agent if he minds if I stop by from time to time to check in. Some agents like you to come by once a month, and others don't. They keep active files and I just have to trust that they are not going to forget me. Obviously, I'm the one who's looking for work so I comply with whatever rules they have about keeping in touch.

Some agents are extremely sensitive to the actors they handle. For others, an actor is just another chip on the roulette board. One actor explained to an interested agent exactly what his "plan" was, what he was interested in pursuing in his acting career. The agent seemed to be listening, but several days later when he called to send the actor on a call, it turned out to be a far cry from the kind of work the actor wanted to do. In this case, the actor crossed the agent off his list. Another actor with an agent who kept sending him on calls for jobs for which he was totally unsuited says, "One was a shoe commercial and I was supposed to be a seventeen-year-old high-school student. I didn't look seventeen at all, and the director laughed when he saw me." Every actor has similar stories about how they have been done in by agents: how agents have tried to make actors do jobs they don't want to do, how they forget about actors and let them do all the work until it's time to collect the 10 per cent, how they give bad advice, and even lie.

On the other hand, if an agent is sincerely interested in

your career, he will work hard for you, pushing and fighting and cutting through the red tape, laying the groundwork for you, negotiating for you, and taking the rejections for you. Like a marriage, your relationship with an agent should be based on some level of trust and mutual interest, and a common understanding of who you are and what you want to do. He should be someone you can communicate with, and someone you feel respects you and your work and your potential.

Here are two final things to remember once you get an agent or manager:

1. There are limits to what an agent can do. It is important that you don't sit around waiting for your agent to make things happen. You must continue to follow through on things that your agent might not have time for or not know about.

2. Don't be too impatient. No matter how hard your agent works for you, it is going to take time for him to establish your presence in the heads of producers and directors. Give him a chance.

AGENCY AGREEMENTS

An agent, or artists' manager as he is frequently referred to in contracts, as defined by the Screen Actors Guild is "a person, co-partnership, association, firm or corporation who or which offers to or does represent, act as the representative of, negotiate for, procure employment for, counsel or advise" an actor in connection with or relating to his employment or his professional career in general. Like any other employment agency, the agent must apply to the state labor commission for a license to practice—to solicit work for his clients and take his 10-per-cent commission from their salaries. The agent or agency must also be franchised: each of the 4A unions (SAG, AFTRA, Equity, AGVA, etc.) will grant a qualified agent a franchise which permits the agent to represent performers in that union. The agent, in turn, is required to use the agency contract which has been approved by the union. This restriction is for the actor's protection, because it insures that an agent cannot represent an actor for terms that are less favorable than those that have been union-approved.

An artist's manager or agency contract (as defined by SAG) is "a contract between an agent and a client providing for the rendition of agency services." The SAG, AFTRA, Equity, and AGVA contracts are fundamentally the same. Each provides that the actor employs the agent to represent him exclusively in a specific area of the business— legitimate theatre, motion pictures, television, etc. The contract specifies the length of the agreement, and the commission that the actor agrees to pay the agent, stating that as long as the agent receives commissions from the actor, the agent shall be obliged to "service" the actor. The contract also includes a date when the actor or agent may terminate the contract for reasons of unemployment, and the name or names of the specific agent or agents who will be available to the actor. In it the agent agrees to maintain telephone service and an office open during reasonable business hours. There is an arbitration clause should any controversy arise under the contract, an outline of the duties of the agent to his client. These agency regulations read as if they were written by the team that does the tax-instruction booklets—highly complicated but so vaguely defined that there is plenty of room for shading.

What Contracts Say

Here are some of their highlights, slightly abridged:

1. To use all reasonable efforts to assist the actor in procuring employment as an actor.

2. To counsel and advise the actor in matters which concern the professional interests of the actor.

3. The agent will be truthful in his statements to the actor.

4. The agent will not conceal facts from the actor which are pertinent and which the actor is entitled to know.

5. The agent will not engage in dishonest and fraudulent practices with regard to the making or entering into of the agency contract or the performance thereof.

6. The agent's relationship will be that of a fiduciary.

7. The agent, when instructed in writing by the actor not to give out information with reference to the actor's affairs, shall not disclose such information.

8. The agent may represent actors of the same general qualifications and eligible to the same parts or roles. The agent agrees that, prior to the execution of the agency contract, he will deliver to the actor on request a list of the actors represented by the agent.

9. The agent shall consider only the interests of the actor in any dealing for the actor.

10. The agent is equipped and shall continue to be equipped to represent the interests of the actor ably and diligently.

11. The agent shall seek and confer with producers and others who may employ or recommend employment of the actor, and read scripts made available to him by the actor.

12. At the written request of the actor, the agent shall give the actor information in writing stating what efforts the agent has rendered on behalf of the actor.

13. The agent shall make no binding commitments without the actor's approval.

14. The agent will not execute a contract for the actor at less than union minimum.

The first exclusive-management contract an actor signs with an agent will be for a period of one year; afterward, the usual term of the contract is three years.

The commission an agent is to receive differs in each union, but it is usually never more than 10 per cent. The SAG contract calls for a straight 10 per cent, while in the Equity contract the commission might, at times, by only 5 per cent, depending upon the amount of money the actor earns each week. In the AFTRA contract there is a provision that the money the actor receives after the agent has deducted his 10 per cent must be at least AFTRA minimum. In other words, if the agent can't get the actor more than scale, he can't take his commission. Most agents, therefore, will ask for "scale plus" which means scale wage plus his 10-per-cent commission.

The circumstances that allow an actor or agent to terminate a contract for reasons of unemployment varies considerably. (A contract cannot be terminated by an actor if the actor has been employed through his own efforts and not the agent's, and the agent can legally take his commission from employment the actor has gotten himself.) Under the Equity contract, if the actor is not employed for two weeks of work during a 120-day period, the contract may be terminated. In the SAG and AFTRA contracts, if the actor fails to be employed for 15 days during any period of 91 days the contract may be terminated, so that the 91-day period is effectively 77; in other words, if an actor has not worked for 77 days, he may end his arrangement with the agent since only 14 days remain and an agent cannot obtain

15 days' employment for the actor in such period. The unemployment period in an AGVA contract is 90 days.

This is a very simplified summary of the basic clauses found in an agency agreement, which are, in fact, much more detailed and complicated in their language. Make sure that you read and understand any contract you sign with an agent, and ask questions about anything that isn't clear to you. A useful book to read in this connection is *What You Should Know About the Contracts You Sign* by Donald C. Faber.

Cameo
New York Agent

This is a small agency. We only handle actors who work in New York and its environs. As you know, most of the work here for actors that makes them money is in commercials—seventy per cent of all commercials are done here, the advertising agencies are here—and soap operas—all but two of the soaps are done in New York.

We are bombarded with new actors all the time, but most of the actors we handle have been referred to us by casting directors at advertising agencies or theatre casting people. Actors do come knocking on the door, and are constantly mailing us their pictures and résumés, but unless something strikes us about the person—something in the picture or the résumé (we do read the résumés and like to see that an actor has had some experience, and we hope that actors don't lie about it)—we file them away. Of course, we don't like to throw them away; they are expensive!

We will not sign an actor willy-nilly. What we usually do if he interests us is start submitting him for jobs and if he starts to go commercially, then we will ask him to sign with us for a year. I must say I hate it when I submit an unsigned actor for a job and find out that he has been submitted by another agent as well. If the first year works out, the next contract will be for a three-year period, although we will not force an actor to stick to a contract with us if he is unhappy. It really doesn't pay, and it's uncomfortable to hold someone in a bind like that against their will.

I think the small agency is definitely better for a newcomer than a large one. The large agency pays the most attention to their big stars, working hardest for them, and putting together big package deals. The small agency can spend more time on the individual actor and on getting his career started.

The last large agency that was really excellent was MCA [Music Corporation of America]. They gave their clients service. But today the big agencies can be cut-throat operations, and an actor can be fired in an instant if he is not making enough money for the agency. There is also competition within the big agencies among actors of the same type. They have even been known to sign an actor just to prevent him from competing with their other clients, to take him out of the running, so to speak.

I have had clients whom I have gotten started leave me to go with a big agency—and then they come back or want to come back to me. This business is cruel enough without an actor having to fight his battles in his agency in addition to competing with a hundred other actors for a part.

Because we are small, we can pay a lot of attention to our clients and give them services as well as getting them jobs. We are like a family—offering father figures, advisers, and psychiatrists for our clients. We *like* our clients and feel a personal connection with them.

I have been in the agency business for quite a few years, and I think that actors are superbeings in some way. They simply have to be to withstand the rejection and abuse that is inherent in this business and survive it.

Cameo
Hollywood Agent

It's a *Catch-22* situation if an actor wants an agent to represent him and doesn't have any film to show. I don't see very many brand-new actors anymore, but of the ones who do manage to get into my office, the first thing I ask is if they have some film on them that I can see. That is what you are selling, after all. Something happens on film to the dimension of an actor; suddenly it gets bigger, it displaces more air; faces change, because a camera will see things that the eyes don't see. But if there is no film to look at, chances are I won't get involved unless the actor intrigues me or I have an instinct about him. If someone comes in and their credits include a lot of work in New York on the stage, I would pay more attention to them because I know what it takes to survive in that town.

Of course, somebody could walk in here or I could see someone in a bit part, and if I was insane about them it really wouldn't matter that he didn't have any film on him. Ali MacGraw could walk in here never having acted in her life, because there is just something going on in her that demands all your attention, and that's a lot of what this business is about. I'm not saying that she is necessarily the most gifted actress around.

Agents who deal exclusively in talent know all the

casting people in town—the television-studio people, the network people, the studio feature people, independent casting directors. And that's where you start with a newcomer if you are starting from scratch. The actor makes those rounds—and then it's time for waiting. I don't find it very productive to send a beginner out on general interviews, although they are done all the time. I would much rather send an actor up for a specific part, even if the project is cast or nearly cast. If I have a focus and can say to a casting director that I have a new person they haven't seen and I know that they want someone with experience but that I think this actor is special, then an impression is made that has a reference point. It will be easier for them to remember that actor in relationship to a certain part they have been working on for months than to have him go up for a Hello-How-old-are-you-Where-are-you-from interview.

I'm handling a girl who has been working for a long time. She worked on the stage in New York and Boston and then she came out here with a play, and then she did a television movie which I saw. I was very impressed by her, and when I met her I had an instinct about her. I said, "This is special." I was then working with Carol Eastman, who had written a movie for Mike Nichols. She described the movie to me, and as she was describing one of the characters, I thought to myself, It can't be true, but this girl is perfect for the part. I told Carol about her, and she thought the girl might be right. Then I got the actress a meeting with Mike Nichols. Coincidentally, the next day they were having the first reading of the script with the two male stars and Mike asked her if she would like to read the part of the girl with them. She did and she was terrific. They were very impressed by her reading, but months went by. It was really torture for her, not only because of the waiting, but also because at that point she was asked to test for a series which meant if she got the series she couldn't do the movie. And we had no reason to believe that she'd get the movie, other than she was right for it. I told her that she might as well test for the series, which she did, but then she got the part in the Nichols picture, the first movie she has made. When I call people about her now, I get leverage from the fact that she's doing the movie; they can figure that if she is good enough for Mike Nichols—which is exactly what I tell them—she's special, and that is how I treat her, and that's how I feel about the people I represent. I wouldn't know how to do it any other way.

When there are shifts within the agency, I have been asked to handle certain people that other agents had been representing. If I don't feel strongly about that person, I've said "no" because they wouldn't mean enough to me; I have too much respect for directors to try and sell them someone I'm not absolutely convinced about. If I don't feel strongly about a person, I can't fight for them. There are agents that do that kind of fighting and are very effective. They can almost bully their way into getting an actor a part. There are times when you see actors give performances which are unbelievably bad and you wonder how they got the part, and sometimes it's selling. There is no doubt about it, some agents are so influential and persuasive that they can talk someone into a talent which simply isn't there.

If an actor gets an agent, he sometimes makes the mistake of thinking that because he is with an agency of this size, he is home free. But it really depends on who the agent is, how his expertise coincides with the actor's qualifications, and how enthusiastic he is. I have seen quite a few people and told them they are making a big mistake if they sign with us. Their names are brought up at staff meetings, and I can tell when it is not going to work. The response is either "no" or "yeah, sure" and I think to myself I wouldn't want to be that actor. I mean everybody will be pulling, but unless there is a "Yes!" from an agent who is going to be pushing and pushing and pushing, as well as reminding the other agents about their client, the actor could conceivably go through life with an agent who says, "I really like you," but nothing will ever happen. The smaller agencies depend upon getting their actors work and so their efforts are going to be relentless. This agency makes most of its living on the stars, the writers, and the directors. And unless an actor is of a certain caliber, he could be passed over.

An agent can be instrumental in an actor's career in that a certain kind of faith in an actor can help put him over the top. There are some personalities that are so strong they will succeed regardless; they will just get themselves into the right place at the right time. But that's very hard to do by yourself. Actors are not, by and large, verbally aggressive people, and much of the time they need an agent to do negotiations for them, as well as take the rejections. There are people in this agency who I think are interesting, and I might be able to get them into a position to see a director or a producer, where another agent might not have done so and this could make a difference in their career. So much of it is luck. But if the talent is there, it will come through. There are an awful lot of actors who don't have the kind of talent that Dustin

Hoffman has, but who do make it on a certain level. And that's because of persistence, timing, and luck.

PERSONAL MANAGERS

The acting business is like a sport. It's like boxing. A manager is in your corner all the time. That's where he's got to be. If he's not in your corner, he ain't in your corner and you haven't got a manager, you've got someone who's ripping you off. He's got to be there when you say "Help! What do I do?"

—AN ACTOR

Unlike agents, personal managers are not required to be licensed by the state, nor do they require a union franchise. Anyone can be a manager—your lawyer, your accountant, your mother, your lover, your spouse. There is, however, an association called the Conference of Personal Managers which has drawn up a standard management contract for the use of the conference's members. It contains the following sentence: "It is clearly understood that you are not an employment agent or theatrical agent or artists' manager; that you have not offered or attempted or promised to obtain, seek or procure employment or engagements for me, and that you are not obligated to do so." In other words, a personal manager cannot legally solicit work for an actor—although there is nothing to stop a manager from calling his friend the producer and casually mentioning that his client is an interesting actor.

A personal manager, as defined by SAG, is "a person, firm or corporation whose services are limited to counseling and advising an actor about and in connection with his professional career." A manager may approve publicity and